METTERNICH

THE AUTOBIOGRAPHY, 1773-1815

Prince Clemens von Metternich

RAVENHALL BOOKS

This edition first published 2004 by Ravenhall Books,

an imprint of Linden Publishing Limited

British Library Cataloguing in Publication Data

Metternich, Clemens, Furst von, 1773-1859
Metternich : the autobiography, 1773-1815
1.Metternich, Clemens, Furst von, 1773-1859 2. Statesmen - Austria -
Biography 3. Austria - Politics and government - 1789-1900
4. Europe - History - 1789-1815
I.Title
943.6'04'092

ISBN 1905043015

Ravenhall Books
Linden Publishing Limited
PO Box 357
Welwyn Garden City
AL6 6WJ
United Kingdom

www.ravenhallbooks.com

Printed and bound in Great Britain
by Creative Print and Design (Wales), Ebbw Vale.

PUBLISHER'S PREFACE

Clemens von Metternich was born in Coblenz on May 15 1773. His father, Count Franz von Metternich-Winneburg, was, unsurprisingly, a diplomat and his mother, Countess Maria von Kagenegg hailed from a distinguished Austrian family.

The young Metternich grew up at the courts of various German princes and it was soon apparent that he had an uncommon talent for tact and style. His father was praising his letters in 1785, writing to his son that:

> 'I am also much pleased by the style of the letter and your handwriting. But, in the first, I wish you to avoid repetitions of thoughts and expressions, and in the latter I desire that you use larger characters.'

In 1788 he was sent to Strasburg to complete his education at the city's famous university. It was a chaotic but exciting time but, at this stage at least, Metternich was not to be distracted from his career by the French Revolution. His first real appointment was at Brussels but he travelled widely in a Europe which was beginning to be convulsed by war and conflict.

In 1795 he was in Vienna, marrying Countess Eleonore von Kaunitz, daughter of a famous diplomat. It was a fortuitous marriage and Metternich soon began to rise through the ranks of the Austrian diplomatic corps. In 1797 he attended the Congress of Rastadt but his first major appointment was to the court of Saxony in 1801 followed by promotion to the court of Berlin. Difficult years lay ahead but Metternich's talents were impressive. In 1806 he achieved considerable success by being posted to Paris as ambassador to Napoleon's court. He charmed and persuaded his way into the hearts and minds of many key figures at Paris, befriending Talleyrand, winning over Caroline Bonaparte and impressing Napoleon. Metternich, however, was less impressed by the French Emperor, finding him poorly dressed and with the uncouth habit of keeping his hat on indoors. However, when Austria rearmed in 1809, Metternich was presented with greater challenges. Placed under arrest he was sent back to Austria, arriving in time to witness Austria's defeat at Wagram. The empire lay weakened, defeated, surrounded by enemies and Metternich was called upon to find the necessary means of salvation.

Metternich's diplomatic opportunism managed to engineer an Austrian bride for a Napoleon looking to divorce Josephine and marry into European royalty. Napoleon opted for Archduchess Marie Louise and Metternich accompanied the young Austrian to Paris in March 1810, noting that she was 'rather plain than handsome in the face, she has a very fine figure and when she is presented properly she will do very well'. Quelling opposition to the marriage at home by winning a few concessions from the French, Metternich followed a pragmatic course of largely abstaining from European alliances whilst being at least nominally aligned with France. Only pressure by Napoleon for Austria to provide troops for his invasion of Russia in 1812 deflected Austria from this comfortable middle ground.

But it was Napoleon's disaster in Russia which forever altered the balance of power in Europe. Metternich used Austria's friendship to bargain with victorious Russia and emergent Prussia, only finally committing Austria to the alliance in June 1813 after a dramatic interview with Napoleon at Dresden. Metternich's attitude towards Napoleon had always been tempered by realism but by 1813 he was saying that:

'Napoleon thinks of me continually, of this I am certain; I must appear to him as some sort of conscience personified.'

Austria joined the fight against Napoleon in August 1813 and was led into the war by an excited Metternich. From that moment on Austria became a key and central power in the alliance which liberated Germany from Napoleon, overthrew the French empire in the Spring of 1814 and set about brokering a peace which would settle the boundaries, status and fate of a Europe emerging from twenty years of incessant warfare.

Prince Metternich (he was created a hereditary prince a day after the French defeat at Leipzig in October 1813) found himself at the height of his influence and, inevitably, the congress convened to settle the affairs of Europe was held in Vienna. In the mass of conflicting influences which gathered at the Austrian capital in 1814 and early 1815, Metternich managed to preserve Austrian influence in Germany whilst restoring large parts of northern Italy to Austrian rule. He also fashioned a concert of European powers and thereby created an instrument which might be used to suppress revolutionary activity across Europe. It was a political system which was to remain in place for decades and it made Metternich a figure of hate for liberals and Europe's greatest statesman for those wishing to preserve the status quo.

Metternich's legacy outlived his death in 1859. Although his final years were blighted by the revolutions of 1848 his reputation grew and he quickly came to personify the model diplomat who cloaks power with charm.

His was a fascinating life in fascinating times. His autobiography covers the period up until 1815 and it was originally published as part of the five-volume set of so-called memoirs in 1880. In fact these memoirs were a collection of documents and fragments from letters rather than recollections as such and the autobiographical memoir is the only substantial peace of first-person writing by Metternich.

The autobiography is made up of three parts. The first was called *Materials for the History of my Public Life* and was written by Metternich in 1844 without a view to publication; the second covers 1810 (there is a break in the narrative at page 133) and was entitled *A Guide to Explain my Manner of Thought*; and the third, which focuses on the years 1813 and 1814 was called *On the History of the Alliances*. These three parts, edited by Prince Richard Metternich were joined together and form a narrative of Metternich's life from 1773 to 1815.

As an account by a man at the very heart of European politics for such a span of time it can not be bettered. This is Clemens von Metternich as he would wish to be seen, calmly steering his state clean through the troubled waters of war and revolution.

CONTENTS

CHAPTER I.

APPRENTICESHIP.

(1773—1800.)

I WAS born at Coblentz in the year 1773, so that my youth coincided with that period which immediately preceded the social Revolution in France, and which served as an introduction to it. Brought up in my father's house with loving care, I grew up under the influences of the position in which I was born,—the public station of my father in the Imperial service, the French social life, and the moral laxity which characterised the smaller German States, before the storm burst forth which was soon afterwards to annihilate them.

At the time of my childhood the educational

methods of Basedow and Campe were in vogue. My first tutor was an aged Piarist. When I was nine years old he died, and he was replaced by another priest, who taught me the *Humaniora* till my thirteenth year, when my father gave me another tutor. Friedrich Simon, born at Strasburg, and a Protestant, had been a teacher in Basedow's philanthropic institution at Dessau. He married a niece of Campe himself, and then, in connection with a Protestant clergyman, Schweighäuser, established an educational institution in Alsace, and afterwards undertook the direction of a similar institution at Neuwied on the Rhine.

Under the guidance of this tutor, I and my brother, who was a year and a half younger than myself, went through the studies of the Gymnasiums till the summer of the year 1788, when we were sent to the University of Strasburg.

This University at that time enjoyed great fame, and was much frequented by Germans, who went thither on account of the facilities it offered for acquiring the German and French languages. The year I went there the youthful Napoleon Bonaparte had just left; he concluded his studies in the artillery regiment quartered at Strasburg. We had the same professors for mathematics and fencing,—a circumstance which was only remembered by those masters when the little artillery officer became, step by step, a great general, First Consul, and afterwards Emperor. During my residence in Strasburg I never heard his name mentioned.* Prince Maximilian of Zweibrücken, afterwards

---

* In passing through Strasburg in 1808, I had a visit from my old fencing-master, Mons. Fustet. ' Is it not a strange thing,'—said he to me, 'that it was ffiy lot to give you fencing-lessons, just after I had given the like to Napoleon? I hope that my two pupils, the Emperor of the French and the

the first King of Bavaria, was colonel of the royal
Alsace regiment then quartered at Strasburg. My
mother, who was intimate with the parents of his wife,
a princess of Hesse-Darmstadt, had recommended me to
the care of this Prince. This charge he fulfilled in the
most cordial manner, and throughout the whole life of
this prince, relations of the utmost confidence existed
between us, which were not without a certain influence
on more than one public occasion.

I left the University of Strasburg in the year 1790,
at the time of the coronation of the Emperor Leopold
at Frankfort, whither my father had summoned me.
The French Revolution was beginning. From that
moment I was its close observer, and subsequently
became its adversary ; and so I have ever remained,
without having been once drawn into its whirlpool. I
have known men whose characters had not sufficient
strength to withstand the misleading glare of innovations and theories, and who have reproached me that
neither my understanding nor my conscience could
sustain themselves at the tribunal of reason and of right.
The errors into which these men fell, I ascribe far
more to weakness of judgment than to the influence of
evil example.

Contingencies which might have drawn me into the
vortex were certainly not wanting. Between the years
1787 and 1790 I was placed under the direction of a
tutor upon whose name the curses of Alsace fell ;
during the Reign of Terror he was a member of the
revolutionary tribunal, over which Eulogius Schneider,
a recreant monk from the diocese of Cologne, presided ;
and he shared in the responsibility of those streams of

Austrian Ambassador at Paris, will not take it into their heads to come to
blows with each other.'

blood shed by that abhorred tribunal in that unhappy province. My religious teacher at Strasburg was Professor of Canon law at the university—and after adopting the civil constitution of the Clergy, had been elected Bishop of Strasburg. Afterwards he foreswore religion and the episcopate, and publicly burned the insignia of his office in a revolutionary orgy. I must do both these men the justice to state, that they never attempted to influence my opinions.

My tutor made himself notorious in Paris on that accursed day, August 10, 1792. It was he who presided over the Council of Ten, which the bandits, known as 'The Marseillaise,' had appointed to conduct the operations of the day. In 1806 I found the same man in Paris again; he was then teacher of the German language in the Collége Louis le Grand, but he afterwards lost that place, being, like all the Jacobins of that time, in disfavour with Napoleon. On the return of the Bourbons, the Duke of Orleans made him German teacher to his children.

The doctrines of the Jacobins and their appeal to the passions of the people, excited in me an aversion, which age and experience have only strengthened. I cherish the conviction that I never should have been at any time, or in the lowest position, accessible to the temptations to which I saw so great a number of my contemporaries yield. I must also admit that the example of the errors, to which an unveracious spirit and the excitement of passion may lead, was not lost upon me; it influenced my own mind, and aided me to avoid the errors into which many fell, only because they had not had the same opportunities of beholding such enormities.

As I have already said, I went to Frankfort in the

year 1790, for the coronation of the Emperor Leopold, where my father was Austrian Ambassador. I was chosen by the Catholic Imperial Courts of the West-phalian Bench to be master of the ceremonies, and I had as colleague, for the Protestant section of the same Bench, Count Friedrich v. Solms-Laubach.

I had only then attained my seventeenth year, and was much flattered by this mark of confidence from so honourable a corporation, functions being assigned to me which, from their important character, seemed to require a man of riper years.

It was in Frankfort that I first came into personal contact with the Archduke, who became afterwards Emperor of Germany under the title of Francis II., and then Emperor of Austria under that of Francis I. He was five years older than I, and had just married his second wife, a Neapolitan princess. On the occasion of the coronation I also made the acquaintance of many eminent persons belonging to the Imperial court and to the best society of Vienna. Although the son of the Emperor's ambassador, I had never yet been in Austria. The only spot of hereditary property on which I had set my foot was the estate of Königswart, where, in the year 1786, owing to the death of Frederic II., I had resided for a short time. In fact, this event recalled my father from his post of Plenipotentiary to the three Rhenish electorates.

The coronation of a Roman emperor at Frankfort was certainly one of the most impressive and splendid spectacles in the world. Everything, down to the most trifling details, spoke to the mind and heart through the force of tradition and the bringing together of so much splendour. Yet a painful feeling overshadowed the marvellous picture then presented by the city of

Frankfort.   A conflagration, which grew with each day,
laid waste the neighbouring kingdom.   Thoughtful men
already saw the influence which this must, sooner or
later, exercise beyond the boundaries of France.   Emigrants also began to pour into the heart of an empire
which had for so many centuries served as a wall of
defence against a movement whose origin must be
sought for long before the outbreak of 1789 ; and this
defensive power itself, too, was already in a condition
of evident decay.   My mind was then too young to be
able to fathom the vicissitudes of that gloomy future ;
absorbed in the present, I saw only, with all the force
of youthful impressions, the contrast between the
country contaminated by Jacobinism, and the country
where human grandeur was united with a noble national
spirit.   Surrounded by a number of dull spectators,
who called themselves the people, I had been present at
the plundering of the Stadthaus . at Strasburg, perpetrated by a drunken mob, which considered itself the
people.   Now I found myself one of the guardians of
public order in a Stadthaus, where so many impressive
ceremonies had taken place, and this at so short a
distance from the great state now in conflagration.   I
repeat it, that I thought only of this contrast, full of
faith in a future which, in my young dreams, was to
seal the triumph of this mighty organisation over
all weakness and error.   I slept close to a volcano,
without thinking of any eruption of lava !

It was towards the end of the residence of the Imperial court in Frankfort that the Emperor Leopold II.
conferred on my father the then very important position
of Minister Plenipotentiary to the States-General of the
Austrian Netherlands.   This title, borrowed from the
diplomatic career, incorrectly described the functions of

the office, the true attributes of which would have been better characterised, if he had been called Prime Minister of the States-General. The popular rising, in which such worthless men as the advocate Vandernoot and a priest of the name of Van Gupen had played so lamentable a part, had just been put down. Following the advice of Prince Kaunitz, who knew his calm wisdom and conciliatory character, my father had been chosen by the Emperor to carry out the moral pacification of those provinces, and this he succeeded in doing, assisted by the repeal of the reforms so unwisely attempted by the Emperor Joseph II.

From Frankfort I went to the University of Mayence, to study Law. My brother, from whom I had never yet been separated, had been, from 1787, placed with me under the care of a clerical tutor, who was an upright, discreet man, and a witness of the errors into which my Jacobin teacher had fallen. I had now concluded my nineteenth year, and, strictly speaking, had no longer a tutor, for my tutor became my friend and counsellor. My residence in Mayence was of the greatest use to me, and had a decided influence on my life. My time was divided between my studies and intercourse with a society as distinguished for intellectual superiority as for the social position of its members. At that time Mayence and Brussels were the *rendezvous* for French emigrants of the higher classes, whose exile was voluntary, not forced as it soon afterwards became, and who had not as yet to struggle with poverty. In my intercourse with the *élite* of this society, I learned to know the defects of the old *régime*; the occurrences, too, of each day taught me, into what crimes and absurdities a nation necessarily falls, when it undermines the foundations of the social edifice. I learned to esti-

mate the difficulty of erecting a society on new foundations, when the old are destroyed. In this way also I
came to know the French; I learned to understand
them, and to be understood by them.

I spent the vacation in the bosom of my family at
Brussels, whither my father had summoned me, that I
might work in his department. The post of Minister
to the States-General was, of all the places which the
Emperor had to bestow, the most important, and at the
same time, one of the most laborious. The minister
united in his own person the chief direction of all the
branches of a substantive government. A numerous
diplomatic corps resided at Brussels, the minister, therefore, found himself at the head of a political cabinet.
The country had just passed through an internal crisis,
the consequences of which were still felt in all directions, so that my position gave me the opportunity to
observe and study at the same time two countries, one
of which was given up to the horrors of the Revolution,
whilst the other still showed fresh traces of what it had
gone through. This position and the instruction I
gained from it have not been lost on me in the long
course of my public life.

With the scenes of devastation before me of which
France was the theatre, my mind naturally turned
towards every study which promised to be most useful
in my future career. I felt that the Revolution would
be the adversary I should have to fight, and therefore
I set myself to study the enemy and know my way
about his camp. I attended the lectures on Law, and
came in contact with professors ·and students of all
shades. As in all German universities, the spirit of
innovation developed itself in Mayence. The progress
of events in France inflamed this disposition. I was

surrounded by students, who named the lectures according to the Republican calendar; and some professors, especially a certain Hofman, who at that time (1792) was head of one of the clubs at Mayence, made it their business to interlard their lectures with allusions to the emancipation of the human race, as it was so well begun by Marat and Robespierre. George Forster, the learned companion of the famous navigator James Cook in his voyages, then living there, gathered round him numerous acolytes of the Revolution. I visited at his house, and saw the effect of the seductive principles to which many youthful minds fell victim. Kotzebue, the dramatist, was also living at Mayence at that time; he was then an ardent follower of a school which, twenty-five years later, turned their daggers against him.

From this epoch date the relations between me and the historian Nicolas Vogt, whose remains are buried on the Johannisberg. I attended his lectures on the History of the German Empire; and whether he guessed how much help I should afterwards obtain from his lectures, or whether from the force of sympathy between us, I always reckoned him among the number of my most zealous friends. Often have I recalled the saying with which he concluded a discussion between us on the subject of historical criticism:—' Your intellect and your heart are on the right road; persevere therein also in practical life, the lessons of History will guide you. Your career, however long it may be, will not enable you to see the end of the conflagration which is destroying the great neighbouring kingdom. If you do not wish to expose yourself to reproaches, never leave the straight path. You will see many so-called great men pass by you with swift strides; let them pass, but do not deviate from your path. You will overtake them, if only because you must meet them on their way back!' The good man was right.

In July 1792, I was present at the coronation of the Emperor Francis, and then performed the same duties as at that of his illustrious predecessor.

The appearance which Frankfort then presented was very different from that of this city two years earlier. France was now bowed beneath the Reign of Terror. Events followed each other in quick succession. The comparison between what was going on in Frankfort and what was taking place in the neighbouring kingdom was too striking to escape notice, and could not but be painfully evident to the mind.

The light-heartedness which characterised the French emigrants assembled in the city for the coronation was in strong contrast with this impression. The princes of the royal family were all gathered together at Coblentz. All who fled from the Revolution reckoned on their exile lasting for two months. Thoughtful men glanced at the Prussian army assembled on the Rhine, and at the war which had already broken out in Belgium, Austria, and France.

Among the personages who greatly attracted my attention in Frankfort, I may mention the Abbé Maury, who officiated here as Papal Nuncio, and Vicomte de Mirabeau, known by the *sobriquet* of Mirabeau-Tonneau, the younger brother of the famous Mirabeau : a man of spirit and great courage, just as enthusiastic in his loyalty as his brother was revolutionary. In the Abbé Maury I did not recognise the fearless deputy of the National Assembly, and for this reason, doubtless, I was the less surprised to meet him a year afterwards as Cardinal and almoner to Princess Pauline Borghese, Napoleon's sister.

In regard to the circumstances, the pageant and ceremonies of this coronation were perhaps of a more imposing character than at the former. Prince Anton Esterhazy, the principal Ambassador of the Emperor, entrusted me in the most friendly manner with the direction of the banquet which he gave after the coronation. I opened the ball with the young Princess Louise of Mecklenberg, who afterwards, as Queen of Prussia, was distinguished for her beauty and noble qualities. She was two years younger than I. We had known each other from childhood, for these young Princesses of Mecklenberg, of whom one was Queen of Prussia and the other Queen of Hanover, were brought up at Darmstadt under the care of their grandmother, who was on intimate terms with my mother. The most friendly relations existed between us during the whole life of that princess.

When the coronation was over, the monarch and most of the German princes departed to Mayence, where the Elector held his court in great luxury, this court being at that time the most luxurious in Germany. The French princes had arrived, everything was ready for the beginning of the campaign. Great hopes were placed on the result, and certain victory was generally expected. The French emigrants thought the undertaking sure of success, and the only complaint they were heard to utter related to unavoidable delays in the assembling of the army. According to their idea, the despatch of a few battalions only was needed, in order that the white flag should immediately appear on all the towers of France.

No doubt these lofty delusions brought about the defeat which the Prussian army soon afterwards sustained.

From Mayence I went to Coblentz, to which place

the French princes returned. The Prussian army had encamped near the village of Metternich, which lies a mile (German) distant from the town. There for the first time I came to know the Crown Prince of Prussia, who, after the death of King Frederick William II., mounted the throne.

Frederick William II. was the picture of a king. In stature he was almost a giant, and stout in proportion. In all assemblies he stood a head taller than the crowd. His manners were stately and pleasant. The emigrants were certain that he had only to show himself on the frontiers, and the *sans-culottes* would lay down their arms. Frenchmen of that day did not at all comprehend the Revolution; and, indeed, I do not believe that, with a few exceptions, they ever succeeded in doing so. But this weakness is not the exclusive property of the French, for people in general do not even guess the true causes or the purpose of events which take place before their eyes.

Soon after this, the campaign commenced and dispelled all these dreams. Defective in organisation, and conducted by a man whose military reputation was founded simply on a flattering speech of Frederick II., it ended in a calamitous retreat. All that I afterwards was able to discover about this campaign left me no doubt whatever that, if the Duke of Brunswick, instead of losing time in Champagne, had marched straight to Paris, he would have effected an entrance into that city. What would have been the consequence of such a success, it is difficult to determine; but for my part, I feel convinced that the Revolution would not have been suppressed. Apart from the fact that the military power was too weak to maintain the first success, the evil had spread to an extent too vast to be re-

strained in its onward steps by merely military operations, and Europe was the victim of so many illusions
beyond the range of the Revolution that moral remedies could not keep pace with the power of the
sword. In the latter part of the summer I went to
Brussels. The war was at its height. My university
studies were interrupted in consequence of these events.
I passed to and fro between Brussels and the army,
sometimes with commissions from my father, sometimes
to visit my friends. On one of these occasions, as I
was returning to Brussels, an adjutant of the general
in command came to inform my father that the commander of the French army, General Dumouriez, had
just seized the commissaries of the Convention, and
sent them to the Austrian outposts. I was deputed to
receive them on their arrival at Brussels. I had many
interviews with them in the prisons which were assigned
to them, and heard their complaints against the general,
whom they had been ordered to remove and imprison.
Shortly after this, we saw General Dumouriez himself
arrive in the Netherlands. The French Reign of Terror
destroyed its own commanders just as cartridges destroyed the soldiers. The execution of Louis XVI. and
of Marie Antoinette had called forth beyond the confines of France, and especially in our army, a horror
which soon passed into implacable hatred, and for some
weeks our troops, in spite of the efforts of the officers,
gave no quarter in battle.

The campaign of the year 1793 concluded with the
capture of Valenciennes. I was present at almost all
the operations of the siege, and had therefore the
opportunity of observing war very closely; and it is
to be wished that all those who are called upon to
take a leading part in the business of the State could

learn in the same school. In the course of my long public life I have often had reason to congratulate myself upon the experience thus gained.

I passed the winter of 1793–1794 in the Netherlands, continuing the studies of the service for which I was destined, and being employed in the business of the Cabinet. Brussels was full of strangers, and the emigrants continued to dream of the end of their exile with a confidence which I was far from sharing.

Towards the end of the winter, Vicomte Desandroins, chief treasurer of the Netherlands Government, was entrusted with a mission to the English Government. I accompanied him to London, and was there received by King George III. with unusual kindness and affability. The relations between the Imperial Court and that of Great Britain were most confidential, and public feeling manifested itself in both countries with the same energy against the horrors of the French Revolution, as indeed their interests seemed to be identical. I thus paid a visit to England under the happiest auspices, and my residence there brought me into contact with the most remarkable men of this great epoch. In this way I came to know William Pitt, Charles Fox, Burke, Sheridan, Charles Grey (afterwards Lord Grey), and many other personages, who then and afterwards played great parts on the theatre of public life. I frequented the sittings of Parliament as much as possible, and followed with particular attention the famous trial of Mr. Hastings. I endeavoured to acquaint myself thoroughly with the mechanism of the Parliament, and this was not without use in my subsequent career. I was then appointed Ambassador Extraordinary and Minister Plenipotentiary of the Emperor at the Hague. This circumstance, being known in

London, procured me admission to a sphere of society generally unapproachable for a young man of one-and-twenty. I came to know the Prince of Wales, afterwards Regent, then at last King, with the title of George IV. Our relations, begun at this time, lasted during the prince's whole life. Great dissensions at this period divided the Royal family of England. The Prince of Wales had taken up the side of the Opposition. My youth restrained me from expressing the profound disapproval which his conduct produced in me; but I took one day the opportunity of saying a word to him on the subject, of which he reminded me thirty years afterwards, and added, ' You were very right then ! '

The Prince of Wales was one of the handsomest men I ever saw, and to an agreeable exterior he added the most charming manners. He possessed a sound intelligence, which alone preserved him from being corrupted by the bad society in which he moved with ease himself, without ever permitting the slightest want of respect in others. He took a great fancy to me, and was pleased, I think, at my reserve in a society which was not agreeable to me.

The war between France and England had meantime broken out, and the moment now drew near when the naval strength of the two powers was to be measured against each other. Several hundred merchant vessels, bound for the East and West Indies, waited in the roads at Spithead and St. Helen's for the opportunity to set sail. A great fleet of men-of-war was to protect the merchantmen from an attack, for which great naval preparations had been made in the harbour of Brest. I eagerly desired to see the sailing of the fleet. When the King heard of this, he was kind enough to order that everything should be done to facilitate the execu-

tion of my purpose; and one day when I waited
on him, he told me he would let me know when to go
to Portsmouth to be present at the departure of the
fleet, and would give the necessary directions to Admiral
Howe and the harbour-master to secure the gratification of my curiosity. Shortly afterwards his Majesty
sent to inform me that the moment for my departure
was come, and furnished with letters to the above-
named officers, I travelled to Portsmouth. This town
was so full of sightseers that, but for the attention of
the naval officers, who had secured lodgings for me, no
such accommodation would have been found. The day
after my arrival I paid the harbour-master a visit, and
went on board the admiral's ship, to present the letters
with which I had been provided. The admiral received
me with the greatest politeness, and assured me he
would have me informed the moment the fleet was ready
to sail.

I spent three days at Portsmouth, in visiting the
different establishments in that town, and in the night
of the third day I was awoke by the news, brought by
an officer sent by Admiral Howe, that he had instructions
to conduct me to the Isle of Wight. From the top of
the hill behind Cowes, we could see the fleets leave the
roads and join company on the other side of the island,
on the south of which a vessel was stationed for my use,
in order to convey me to the admiral's ship. We left
Portsmouth immediately, and landed on the Isle of
Wight in the early morning, reaching our point of
observation about six o'clock in the morning. A fresh
breeze sprang up, and this was the signal for the departure of more than four hundred ships. I consider
this the most beautiful sight I have ever seen, I might
say, indeed, the most beautiful that human eyes have

ever beheld! At a signal from the admiral's ship the merchantmen unfurled their sails, the fleet for the West Indies turned to the west, the fleet for the East Indies passed to the east side of the island, each accompanied with a portion of the royal fleet. Hundreds of vessels and boats, filled with spectators, covered the two roads as far as the eye could reach, in the midst of which the great ships followed one another, in the same manner as we see great masses of troops moved on the parade ground. Four French men-of-war, coming from Toulon, with emigrants on board, hoisted the white flag and joined the English fleet. This circumstance, unparalleled in the annals of history, gave a character to the occurrence which will never fade from the memory of those who witnessed it. In a few hours the two fleets met to the south of the island. As soon as my guide gave the signal for departure, we descended the hill and joined Admiral Howe on board the 'Queen Charlotte.' I remained with the admiral, who loaded me with attentions, till the evening of May 30.

A despatch boat sent from the English fleet of observation before Brest brought the news that the French fleet had set sail and put out to sea. In spite of my earnest petitions to the admiral to allow me to remain to see the great events which were imminent, he obliged me to leave him: 'The King told me,' said he, ' to let you see everything ; but I have to send you back alive, and cannot take upon myself to expose you to the dangers of a sea-fight.' With the greatest regret, therefore, I left the fleet, and went on board the vessel which the admiral was sending off to Portsmouth with his despatches to the Admiralty ; and after a few days' stay in Portsmouth, I returned to London. The city I found illuminated, and the people

filled with rapture at the news of the great naval victory
of the 1st of June off Ushant. This news preceded me by a few hours only. I remained in London two days; and on the third I travelled back to
Portsmouth, to see the arrival of the fleet with their
prizes.

The admiral's ship, which I had left a few days
before in the most perfect condition, was one of those
which suffered the most severely. She had joined
battle with the French admiral's ship, and presented the
appearance of a ruin; the greater part of her crew had
been killed or disabled. Admiral Howe, who to my great
joy escaped unhurt, returned covered with laurels.

I was to have returned to the Netherlands in the
middle of summer, but the war prevented me; and
while waiting to see how events would turn out, I visited
the interior of England. At the commencement of the
autumn, as the enemy had entered the Netherlands, I
embarked at Harwich to cross over to Helvoetsluys.
We were overtaken by a heavy gale, which drove us
into the roads of Dunquerque, just as that town was
being bombarded by Sir Sidney Smith. I was exposed
to a cross fire for more than two hours, and had only
to thank a sudden change of wind for my escape from
so dangerous a position. From this circumstance a
report was started and disseminated by the newspapers
of the day that I had been taken prisoner by the
French. This false report reached the ears of my
father, and he, with the commander-in-chief of the
Austrian army, was just on the point of approaching
the French Government with regard to my liberation,
when he heard of my landing in Holland. I remained
in this country so long as was necessary to enable me
to visit the Hague, Amsterdam, and part of North

Holland, and from thence I repaired to the seat of government of the Netherlands on the Lower Rhine, to which place it had retired.

In the beginning of October I travelled with my father to Vienna, and visited that capital for the first time. In the month of February of the same year Prince Kaunitz died, and the direction of foreign affairs was entrusted to Baron von Thugut. I had made his acquaintance in Brussels, where he passed several months with Count Mercy d'Argenteau, who lived in the Belgian capital after his return from his post of ambassador in Paris. I have already mentioned that I had been chosen for the mission to the Hague; but after the conquest of Holland by Pichegru's army, it did not suit me to take that post, and I waited the development of events, without impatience, but with a feeling of bitterness against the Revolution the consequences of which threatened the whole body of society. The left bank of the Rhine was occupied by the troops of the French Republic. Those were to blame for this blow who had so utterly mistaken the strength and extent of the Revolution. The greater part of our family estates lying on the left bank of the Rhine had been confiscated by the *great nation*; it was necessary, therefore, to turn to the estates we had in Bohemia, which had brought in but little to my father, or his predecessors during the last century, but which had now to be made the most of. My father sent me thither in order to carry out the necessary measures on the spot. I spent the months of November and December alone in Königswart, and occupied myself with the management of the affairs entrusted to me.

On my return to Vienna, I found my parents busy with a project for my marriage. Prince Ernst Kaunitz, eldest son of the chancellor, had an only daughter; he had become acquainted with me during my first short residence in Vienna. Preliminary conferences between the parents made the conclusion of the marriage dependent on the mutual inclinations of the young people. I was only one-and-twenty, and the thought of marrying so young had never occurred to me. It was soon evident to me that my parents much desired this marriage; but as the Princess Kaunitz shortly afterwards had an illness, from which she only recovered in March 1795, I did not make the acquaintance of my bride-elect till the summer, and our betrothal was arranged to take place in the autumn of the same year.

Prince Ernst Kaunitz loved his daughter tenderly, and was determined not to part with her, so that I consented that we should live with him. The betrothal was celebrated on September 27, 1795, at Austerlitz, the place which ten years afterwards became so sadly famous.

I have already said that the public service presented no attractions for me. I had determined to remain in private life, and to devote my time to the cultivation of learning and science. At the time of which I speak fortune seemed to favour my inclinations, and I made a plan for myself, which I was not permitted to carry out.

I must also acquaint my readers with other causes which kept me aloof from public affairs. Still young, and placed in a position which allowed me to observe, from the highest point of view, the course of the greatest events, I found that they were not conducted as they ought to have been. '*Les affaires ce sont les hommes*;' affairs are only the expression of the faculties or the weaknesses of men, of their inclinations and their errors, their virtues and their vices. Inaccessible to prejudice, and seeking only the truth in everything, my modesty did not allow me to find fault with persons in power if I was not satisfied with what I saw; on the contrary, I ascribed to the weakness of my own understanding and to my inexperience the feeling which forced me to disapprove of the course they had taken. But neither inclination nor duty led me to acquire the necessary experience. My particular vocation seemed to me to be the cultivation of knowledge, especially of the exact and physical Sciences, which suited my taste particularly. I loved the fine arts too, so that nothing aroused in me any desire to put my freedom into fetters. The diplomatic career might certainly flatter my ambition, but during all my life I have never been accessible to this feeling.

In the autumn of 1797, death carried off my father-in-law. Home duties and study continued to be my occupation. I diligently attended lectures on Geology, Chemistry, and Physics; then too, as afterwards, I followed with attention the progress of Medical Science. Man and his life seemed to me to be objects worthy of study. Vienna had for many years been rich in great physicians. Van Swieten and Stoll were dead; the first professorial chair was filled by Peter Franck; Quarin did honour to science by his extensive knowledge; Gall continued his lectures to a select audience; Jacquin was continually making fresh advances in botany. I was happy in this scientific circle, and allowed the Revolution to rage and rave without feeling any call to contend with it. It pleased Providence afterwards to rule quite otherwise.

The Congress of Rastadt drew me out of my retirement. The Counts of the Westphalian 'Collegium' entrusted me with the care of their interests. I undertook the charge, more from a feeling of duty than in the hope of being able to serve a body whose existence was threatened, as was that of the German Empire itself. I remained in Rastadt till the middle of March 1799. As the dissolution of the Congress approached, I took my wife and daughter back to Vienna. A short time after my return to this capital, I learned the catastrophe which signalised the end of a Congress which, from beginning to end, had been but a phantom. I had no opportunity at that time of seeing Bonaparte. He had left Rastadt two days before my father and I arrived. In their respective capacities of First Plenipotentiary of the Empire and of the French Republic, my father and Bonaparte had their apartments in the Palace of the city, separated only by the great saloon.

Returning home, I again resumed my own manner of life and my accustomed employments. My stay in Rastadt only strengthened me in my opposition to a career which in no wise satisfied my mind and disposition. The French Revolution had reached and passed the climax of its barbarous follies ; the Republic was only the miserable dregs of it; and a disunited Germany was paralysed by the peace which Prussia had separately concluded with France at Basle, and by the system of neutrality at any price, which the Princes of North Germany had adopted. Austria alone was in the field, and the war was badly carried on. Was there anything in such a situation to summon me to exchange my peaceful life for a life of activity constrained to move within limits conflicting with my spirit of independence and cramping my conscience?

These feelings of mine might easily give the impres-

sion that my temper had become morose. But that
would be a mistake. I was preserved from this weakness by my love for grave studies. I never shut myself
up from the world ; my life was that of a man who
sought exclusively good society ; this alone had any
power of attraction for me. The day was usually given
entirely up to business, and the evening was divided
between work and recreation. I frequented those
salons by preference in which I was sure to find pleasant conversation, convinced that such conversation
serves to sharpen the intellect, correct the judgment,
and is a source of instruction to those who know how
to keep it from degenerating into mere babbling.

At that time there were in Vienna several foreigners
remarkable for their intellectual gifts ; among whom
I may particularly mention Pozzo di Borgo, who afterwards played a great part in public affairs. He was at
that time employed as a secret agent by the English
Cabinet. I met him often in society. I remarked in him
an extraordinary fluency combined with southern warmth
in expressing his feelings. One *salon*, with which, however, I had only a distant connection, was that of the
Prince de Ligne's. The Prince himself was conspicuous
for the peculiar quickness of his intellect ; and his *salon*
was frequented by a very mixed company, of whom the
greater part affected the reputation of wits, without
being particularly intellectual. For many years the
Prince had honoured me with especial kindness. During
my residence in the Netherlands he had wished to
bestow on me his second daughter in marriage, and
used to call me his son-in-law, a name which he continued to give me in joke as long as he lived. The
conquest of the Netherlands brought the Prince and
his family from Brussels to Vienna. By a strange caprice

of fortune, the Prince's daughter, who had been destined for me, married a Count Pallfy, who had been at one time engaged to marry the very daughter of Prince Kaunitz, who became my wife.

The house which I most frequented was that of the Princess Liechtenstein, an aunt of my wife on the mother's side, and one of those five princesses who for many years were the intimate friends of the Emperor Joseph II. This small circle, known during the reign of this monarch by the name of 'the Society of Princesses,' consisted of Princess Franz Liechtenstein, Princess Ernest Kaunitz and her sister, Princess Karl Liechtenstein, and the Princesses Kinsky and Clary. Of men, besides the Emperor Joseph, there were Marshal Lascy, Lord-in-waiting, Count, afterwards Prince, Rosenberg, and the Prince de Ligne. After the death of the Emperor, this society was dispersed. The Princess Karl gathered around her the remains of this circle of all that Vienna possessed of persons distinguished for their agreeable manners. The Countess Rombec too, sister of Count Ludwig Cobenzl, then ambassador at St. Petersburg, opened her *salon*; which was much frequented by foreigners and especially by French emigrants.

I had arranged to pass the winter in the capital, and the summer months in the country, sometimes in Moravia on an estate belonging to my wife, sometimes in Bohemia on one belonging to my family. I had entirely withdrawn myself from public affairs, and in regard to them I was simply a spectator. The result of my observations was not favourable to the cause which all my life I have considered that of reason and right. From time to time I visited Baron Thugut, who in his capacity of Minister of Foreign Affairs conducted the affairs of the Imperial Chancellerie.

I have already mentioned our previous acquaintance. I made no attempt to come into closer intimacy with him; nothing urged me to it, for I wanted no place, and Baron Thugut had no relations, beyond his official duties, with anyone. I agreed with him in his principles, but not with the manner in which he carried them out, and the results of his ministry have proved only too thoroughly that I was right.

Sometimes I waited on the Emperor, who let no opportunity slip of reproaching me with what he called my indolence. One day when I had been speaking of my views on this subject, he said to me, ' You live as I should be very happy to live in your place! Hold yourself ready for my orders, that is all I expect of you for the present.'

Young Metternich, a lithograph by F. Lieder.

CHAPTER II.

ENTRANCE INTO POLITICAL LIFE.

(1801—1803.)

Thugut's character and resignation—Cobenzl—Enters the public service—
Conversation with the Emperor—As ambassador at Dresden—Beginning
of public life—Leading motives—Arrival at Dresden—Mr. Elliot—
Dresden as a post of observation for the Northern courts—Fabrication
of diplomatic correspondence.

WITH the conclusion of the Peace of Luneville (1801)
the weakness and vacillations of the Austrian Cabinet
reached their height.   During a conflict of ten years
the policy of the Imperial court had raised a barrier,
sometimes stronger, sometimes weaker, to the destructive principles of all the Governments of France which
had succeeded one another since 1792.   But the opposition so offered, betrayed only too much the utter want
of consistency of plan.   In this lay the great defect of
the Cabinet, to whom also it has been ascribed, that the
successes achieved one day were destroyed on the next.
More than to all other causes, France owed her enormous successes to the inconsistent action of the
ministries who conducted affairs from the death of the
great statesman who for forty years presided over the
cabinet of Vienna, but who, alas! had latterly suffered
from the infirmities of age.   The views upon which the
policy of Austria was always based could not be conceived more clearly than they were, but never was
their execution more feebly carried out.

The ministry of Baron Thugut displays nothing but an unbroken series of mistakes and miscalculations. When he was at the height of his power, he was distrusted by two parties, each from its own standpoint, in exactly opposite directions. He was accused by the one of having sold himself to France; others pretended that England had him in her pocket. It is to be deplored, both for his own sake and for Austria's, that no one has ventured to assert that Thugut had served the interests of his country and not his own.

Although we never attributed the political attitude of Thugut to foreign influence, it never occurred to us to trace it to treachery, which is always the most dangerous and generally a precarious means of success.

Sprung from a mean condition, the son of a mariner at Linz, Thugut was educated in the Oriental Academy, and trained for subordinate service in the state. Subtle and dexterous, he owed the success of his political career to these qualities, which, when supported by deep dissimulation and a love of intrigue, pass only too easily for real talents.

He had invested the greater part of the property which he had acquired at Constantinople in the French funds, and without doubt it was anxiety for the preservation of this property which at the time of the outbreak of the Revolution blinded him, or at least kept him inactive. Then it was that the suspicion arose in the English party that he had been gained over to France. When however the Reign of Terror destroyed every spark of hope of saving even the smallest portion of his property from the general bankruptcy, Thugut, less restrained, changed his policy; hence it came about that the public, observing this change, took up the idea that it had been brought about by English gold.

Not without talent, robed in the highest dignity of the state, living in the obscurity of retirement and yet with cold and calculating ambition interfering with all the branches of the government, Thugut was inaccessible to bribery and corruption.   The history of his ministry may be summed up in a series of miscalculations, all of which contributed to support and advance the preponderance of France.

In consequence of the Peace of Luneville Thugut retired from the public service.   Count Cobenzl was recalled from St. Petersburg, and appointed to the direction of Foreign Affairs.   The first Lord-in-waiting, Count, afterwards Prince, Trautmannsdorf, held the portfolio provisionally.   The peace with France necessarily gave a new impulse to Austrian diplomacy.

The posts in London, Berlin, and St. Petersburg were already filled.   There were ambassadors at Stockholm, and some of the smaller courts of Germany and Italy.   The Emperor felt it necessary to fill up the gaps which Thugut, according to the custom which he sometimes carried too far, had left open.   Occupied solely with the war against the French Revolution, Thugut paid no attention to anything that did not seem to him immediately connected with that war. Hence it happened that he did not read and consequently did not answer the despatches of embassies of the second rank.   When removed from the Ministry, a commission had to be appointed to open and place in the archives hundreds of the reports and letters sent from such embassies.

A few days after he had taken office, Count Trautmannsdorf summoned me to him, and informed me that the Emperor, when he resolved to fill up the places mentioned above, had ordered him to give me the choice between the post at Dresden or Copenhagen, or to remain at home as Minister for Bohemia to the German Reichstag. I begged him to allow me to think over the matter, and betook myself to the Emperor. I laid before his Majesty openly my ideas as to my future life, and the talents I believed myself to possess, and those which I could not lay claim to. The Emperor received my professions with his accustomed kindness; but when he appealed to my patriotism, I yielded to his will. 'Your Majesty,' said I, 'desires that I should enter a sphere for which I believe I have no vocation; I submit to your commands. I pray your Majesty never to doubt my will, but to distrust my capabilities. I will make the experiment, and your Majesty will permit me to retire from the service when, as I fear, the day comes that I shall not answer your expectations.' The Emperor answered with a smile: ' He who cherishes such fears is not in danger of injuring the public service. I promise you to be the first to tell you if I find you on the wrong road.'

I decided for the embassy in Dresden. Denmark seemed to me too remote, and it was repugnant to me to go to Regensburg only to witness the obsequies of the noble German Empire. Dresden, on the contrary, one stage on the way to Berlin or St. Petersburg, I valued as a post of observation which might be made useful. Having been constrained to adopt this career, I desired at any rate to have the prospect of being useful. I could never do anything by halves; once a diplomatist, I determined to be one thoroughly, and in the sense which I connected with diplomacy. Subsequent events showed that I reckoned rightly, for, the path once entered, events hurried me along it only too swiftly.

Here, at the commencement of the account of **my**

public life, I propose to admit into the narrative only what relates to myself, or rather what may serve to fill up the gaps in the official correspondence; for although the latter alone gives a true picture of the work of a statesman, yet in such documents many details find no place. I wish that those of my readers who may be in a position to have access to the Imperial archives may consult the documents of the time in connection with the present work; and, drawing from this double source, they will more easily appreciate the great epoch during which destiny had laid upon me the difficult task of playing an active part on the world's stage. But before I relate the many remarkable occurrences which have signalised my career, I will candidly state the principles on which the actions of my political life have been based. This statement will serve to clear up many points in the history of my time and explain my own actions.

That a public career was distasteful to me I have already mentioned. Convinced that everyone ought to . be prepared to answer for the deeds of his own life; penetrated by the consciousness of the enormous difficulties of propping up a society which was falling to pieces on every side; disapproving, before the tribunal of my own conscience, of almost all the measures which I saw adopted for the salvation of the social body, undermined as it was, by the errors of the eighteenth century; lastly, too diffident to believe that my mind was of so powerful a stamp that it could improve whatever it undertook: I had determined not to appear on a stage on which the independence of my character rebelled against playing a subordinate part, though I did not consider myself capable of taking the part of a reformer.

The care with which my education had been directed to the wide field of politics had early accustomed me to contemplate its vast extent. I soon remarked that my mode of thinking of the nature and dignity of this sphere was essentially different from the point of view from which all this was regarded by the enormous majority of those who are called to play great political parts. Here I may be allowed to propound the few principles to which I have always reduced the science commonly known by the name of Politics and Diplomacy.

Politics is the science of the vital interests of states. Since, however, an isolated state no longer exists, and is found only in the annals of the heathen world, or in the abstractions of so-called philosophers, we must always view the society of nations as the essential condition of the present world. Thus, then, each state, besides its separate interests, has also those which are common to it with other states. The great axioms of political science proceed from the knowledge of the true political interests of all states. In these general interests lies the guarantee of their existence, while individual interests to which the transitory political movements of the day assign a great importance, and the care of which constitutes political wisdom in the eyes of a restless and short-sighted policy, possess only a relative and secondary value. History teaches us that whenever the separate come into conflict with the general interests of a state, and the latter are neglected or mistaken in the zealous and extensive prosecution of the former, this is to be regarded as an exceptional or unhealthy condition, whose development or speedy amendment ultimately decides the destiny of the state, that is, its impending decline or its recuperative prosperity. That which characterises

the modern world, and essentially distinguishes it from
the ancient, is the tendency of nations to draw near to
each other, and in some fashion to enter into a social
league, which rests on the same basis with the great
human society developed in the bosom of Christianity.
This foundation consists of the precept of the Book of
books, 'Do unto others as ye would they should
do unto you.' This fundamental rule of every human
fraternity, applied to the state, means in the political
world reciprocity, and its effect is what in the language
of diplomacy is called *bons procédés*, in other words,
mutual consideration and honourable conduct. In the
ancient world, policy isolated itself entirely, and exercised the most absolute selfishness, without any other
curb than that of prudence. The law of retaliation
set up eternal barriers and founded eternal enmities
between the societies of men ; and upon every page of
ancient history is found the principle of mutual evil for
evil. Modern history, on the other hand, exhibits the
principle of the solidarity of nations and of the balance
of power, and furnishes the spectacle of the combined
endeavours of several states against the temporary pre-
dominance of any one to impede the extension of this
principle, and to constrain it to return to the common
law. The establishment of international relations upon
the basis of reciprocity, under the guarantee of respect
for acquired rights, and the conscientious observance of
plighted faith, constitutes, at the present day, the essence
of politics, of which diplomacy is only the daily application. Between politics and diplomacy there exists, in my
opinion, the same difference as between science and art.
Just as men daily transgress the laws of civil society,
nations only too often act in opposition to the eternal
precepts which govern their alliance. The faults of

mcn and the faults of states are subject to the same punishments; their whole difference lies in the gravity of the offence, which is proportionate to the importance of the individuals.

When we master these truths, what becomes of a selfish policy, of the policy of fantasy, or of the policy of miserable greed, and especially what becomes of that which seeks profit apart from the simplest rules of right; which mocks at the plighted word, and, in short, rests solely on the usurpations of force or craft?

After this confession of faith, it may be conceived what I have always thought of politicians of the stamp or, if we will, of the authority of a Richelieu, a Mazarin, a Talleyrand, a Canning, a Capo d'Istria, or a Haugwitz, and of many more or less famous names. Resolved not to walk in their steps, and despairing of opening a path in harmony with my own conscience, I naturally preferred not to throw myself into those great political affairs, in which I had far more prospect of succumbing materially than of succeeding: I say materially, for I have never been afraid of failing morally. The man who enters public life has always at command a sure resource against this danger, that is—retirement.

It was in January 1801 that I was made Ambassador Extraordinary and Minister Plenipotentiary to the Electoral Court of Saxony. Peace had just been concluded between France and Austria at Luneville when I entered on my duties at Dresden, towards the end of that year. Napoleon Bonaparte was First Consul of the French Republic, which now existed only in name. The German Empire visibly approached its dissolution. The Emperor Paul had died a violent death in the March of that year. Europe was in a state of extreme tension, the natural result of the uncertainty then hanging over the whole

world.   Dresden, and especially the Electoral court,
like an oasis in the desert, formed a contrast to the
universal agitation.   To judge from this court alone,
one might have believed the world was standing still.
Everything there was ordered and arranged just as the
last Augustus had left it to his successors.   If etiquette,
costume, and precise regulations could be a solid
foundation for a kingdom, then Electoral Saxony would
have been invulnerable.   The costumes of the court, the
gala days, and all its customs, were at that time what
they had been in the middle of the eighteenth century.
The French Revolution, after overthrowing the old monarchy, had reached the stage of Bonaparte's consulate,
but at the Saxon court hoops had not yet been discarded!

The Elector, Frederick Augustus, was a prince of
solid ability, and his government would have long remained a blessed memory to his quiet, and industrious
country had not the storm which a few years later burst
forth destroyed his mild and peaceful rule.

Dresden had always a numerous diplomatic corps.
Among my colleagues, Mr. Elliot, the English ambassador, was conspicuous for the originality and eccen-
tricity of his character.   The life of this diplomatist had
been remarkable.   As a young militia officer, he introduced himself into the great world in a very odd way.
At the reviews at Potsdam a number of foreign officers
gathered every year round King Frederick II.   On these
occasions this prince showed his partiality for the
French, hence the Chamberlain, who had to present
the foreigners at the Prussian court, introduced the
French officers singly by name, while the English officers
were all presented *en bloc*.   At a reception of this kind,
at which young Elliot was present, when the chamberlain said to the king, ' I have the honour to present

to your Majesty twelve Englishmen,' he was interrupted by Elliot, exclaiming in a loud voice, as he turned to leave the room, 'You are mistaken, Herr marschal; there are only eleven.' Some years afterwards Elliot came as Ambassador Extraordinary to Berlin. Frederick had not forgotten the scene at Potsdam, and was little pleased by the appointment of Elliot, who had then only the rank of major. He determined to let his ill-humour with the London court and its representative be seen, and chose a Count Lusi for the post in London. Count Finkenstein was requested to notify this appointment to the English ambassador, which he did in the following words: 'The King has chosen Count Lusi, a major in his army, whose name may be known to you from the reputation he gained in the Seven Years' War. His Majesty flatters himself that your Court will be satisfied with this choice.' Elliot answered without hesitation: 'The King, your master, evidently could not have chosen anyone who would have better represented him.' With such manners as these, Mr. Elliot was not likely to make himself a favourite in Prussia.

Soon after Elliot was recalled from Berlin, and was appointed to Copenhagen, where he, on his own responsibility, declared war with Denmark, with the intention of freeing the King of Sweden from the danger to which he was exposed, by the taking of the fortress of Gothenburg. By this stroke of genius he did indeed attain his object, but nevertheless lost, and certainly with good reason, his second post, and. came to Dresden, where he had already been for some years English ambassador, when I arrived there.

By that time he had somewhat toned down, but he still possessed an extraordinary vivacity and this gained for him a position quite unusual in social life. A plea-

santer man in society I have never known; with a
character of the same mould as that of the Prince de
Ligne, he was in no respect inferior to him, nay, in
many was his superior. I saw him very often during
my residence in Dresden, and reckon my relations with
him among my most pleasant memories. Having a
numerous family, he was anxious to obtain a good
position, and succeeded in getting the appointment of
Governor of Barbadoes, which post he afterwards exchanged for that of a Governor in India, and held
the appointment till his death at a very advanced age.

The Dresden Embassy was interesting as a post
of observation of the Northern courts, and thither I
turned my eyes, and I can testify to the truth that in
diplomacy no post is unimportant. I was careful to
give my court exact intelligence of what I observed,
without having recourse to the expedient for obtaining
news resorted to by my friend Elliot, who when I asked
him one day, how he contrived to have a letter to send to
London every post-day (there were two in the week),
replied: 'You will see no difficulty in the matter when
I tell you my secret; if anything comes to my knowledge which may interest my government, I tell it; if I
do not know of anything, I invent my news, and contradict it by the next courier. You see I can never be
at a loss for material for my correspondence.'

This joke was quite in Mr. Elliot's manner; but it is
not unusual to meet with diplomatic correspondence
made up after the same recipe, not perhaps purposely
invented, but from credulity. This failing arises from
weakness of judgment and the want of a critical examination of facts, which in no branch of the public
service is more necessary than in a diplomatic career.

Louise, Queen of Prussia.

Frederick (III), King of Prussia.

Francis, Emperor of Austria.

CHAPTER III.

I REMAINED at Dresden as ambassador till 1803, when
Count Stadion was appointed Ambassador in St. Petersburg, and I succeeded him at Berlin.

In the same year the Franco-Russian mediation took
place at Regensburg, in consequence of which Germany
experienced a revolution which destroyed the last foundations of the old German Empire, and thus greatly accelerated the moment of its utter dissolution. During
the whole negotiation my father remained in Regensburg, to watch over the interests of his family. He
received as compensation for the loss of his hereditary
estates on the left bank of the Rhine, which had been
confiscated by the French Republic, the Abbey of

Ochsenhausen, and to this new possession I repaired in the course of the summer with my family.

The Emperor had raised Ochsenhausen to be a principality, as he had also raised the title of several other Counts of the Empire, in order to create new votes, and thus to supply the place in the Reichstag of those votes which had been abolished by the secularisation of the ecclesiastical principalities. My father hoped that his love of the fatherland would find an opportunity in the immediate future of contributing to the strengthening of the Empire. I was so far from entertaining this hope, that I had, on the contrary, the firm conviction that the grand creation of Charlemagne was tending inevitably to its end. With its foundations utterly shattered by the process of mediatisation, the Empire even at that time no longer existed, and I saw its elements dissipated, and the impossibility of its cohesion. My presentiments were only too just: and events soon proved this.

When I left Ochsenhausen I went first to Vienna in order to prepare myself for my new mission, and then in December of the same year to Berlin.

My *début* there was easy. I was received by King Frederick William III., and by the Queen as an old friend. The strict etiquette, by which the diplomatic corps was kept at the greatest possible distance from the Prussian court, was observed with regard to me only on those occasions when an exception made in my favour might have had the appearance of referring to my public position, and would therefore have mortified the whole diplomatic body. Eleven years had passed since I had seen the Queen; I found her surrounded with a true halo of beauty and dignity.

Queen Louisa was endowed with the rarest qualities.

She did not excel in what is commonly called *esprit*, but she possessed a refined tact and strength of mind, for the exercise of which in a few years she had only too many opportunities. It would be difficult to describe the dignity and grace of her bearing, or the impression of sweetness and tenderness her manners made.

The royal family were then divided into different households: in the King's were included the widows of Prince Henry and Prince Ferdinand, brothers of Frederick II. The Prince of Orange, husband of a sister of the reigning king, lived in Berlin; and the Princess, wife of Prince Anton Radziwill, also enjoyed the honours of royalty. The Princes Ludwig and August, sons of Prince Ferdinand, had no separate household.

When I arrived in Berlin, Count Haugwitz, Minister of Foreign Affairs, and Baron, afterwards Prince, Hardenberg, exercised a great influence on politics. Freiherr von Stein was Minister of Finance. Of these statesmen I shall often have to speak.

In the diplomatic body there was no man of pre-eminent ability. M. de Laforest, who formerly acted as plenipotentiary in the conference at Regensburg, filled the post of French Ambassador. Herr von Alopäus had been for many years the Russian Ambassador in Berlin, and Mr. Jackson represented England.

Prussia was then in a state of transition. Without attracting attention, this power raised itself from the state of torpor into which it fell through the Peace of Basle, and from the system of neutrality which made Prussia a mere spectator in the wars carried on by Austria and England, and partially by Russia against the French Revolution. A reaction was preparing in the mind of the nation, and especially in the army of

Prussia, which aimed at making a stand against the progressive enlargement of the power of France, now become an empire. A crisis was at hand, produced by the prospect of a new war between Austria and France. By the greater part of the political prophets the camp at Boulogne was regarded as a preparation for a landing in England. Some better instructed observers saw in this camp a French army held in readiness again to cross the Rhine—and that was my opinion.*

Everything accordingly pointed to a renewal of the war. The Prussian cabinet, led by Count Haugwitz and Herr Lombard, dreaded the event; not so the men of action in the army, at the head of whom Prince Louis Ferdinand was specially conspicuous. These were urgent for war, and loudly declared for the interference of Prussia. Berlin was accordingly divided into two camps, which displayed no great tenderness for each other. And here I would say a few words about Prince Louis Ferdinand.

That prince possessed great qualities, which were enhanced still further by a brilliant exterior, a noble

* In one of my longer conversations with Napoleon in the journey to Cambray, whither I accompanied the Emperor in 1810, the conversation turned upon the great military preparations which he had made in the years 1803–1805 in Boulogne. I frankly confessed to him that even at that time I could not regard these offensive measures as directed against England. 'You were very right,' replied the Emperor, smiling; 'never would I have been such a fool as to make a descent upon England, unless indeed a revolution had taken place within that country.. The army assembled at Boulogne was always an army against Austria. I could not place it anywhere else without giving offence, and being obliged to form it somewhere, I did so at Boulogne, where I could whilst collecting it also disquiet England. The very day of an insurrection in England, I should have sent over a detachment of my army to support the insurrection; I should not the less have fallen on you, for my forces were echelonned for that purpose. Thus you saw in 1805 how near Boulogne was to Vienna.'

bearing, and refined manners. Of quick apprehension and clear intellect, Prince Louis Ferdinand united in himself all that goes to make a remarkable man. Unhappily evil company had too much influence on his life. There were in him two different men : the one capable of everything great and noble ; the other, regardless of these gifts of nature. I had much to do with this prince, who even took a liking for me, but the defects which I have mentioned raised a barrier between us. All my life I have had a horror of low company, but the prince was surrounded with it. In political principles we agreed, but our tastes and our manner of life differed too much for any true confidence to be possible between us.

The year 1804 passed in that unhappy condition which is neither peace nor war. The heavens were covered with thunder-clouds, the first flash from which did not issue until 1805.

In Austria great preparations were being made for a campaign. Count Ludwig Cobenzl was Vice-Chancellor ; he and Count Colloredo, cabinet minister, were regarded as the leaders of the policy of the Empire. Count Colloredo was no great statesman ; Count Cobenzl, a candid, open-hearted man, had, in his capacity of the Emperor's ambassador at the court of Catherine II. lived for many years in confidential intercourse with her—a favour which he shared with the Prince de Ligne, Count Ségur, the French envoy, and other excellent men, whom that princess liked to assemble around her. Although he shone in the *salon*, Cobenzl was not the man to lead a cabinet. Taught by the defeats of the earlier campaigns, and convinced by experience that the means applied in those campaigns were insufficient, and that Napoleon must be met by

other generals than those who held the command in preceding wars, the Emperor had singled out General Mack,
who stood high in the estimation of the army.   Events
afterwards proved how unhappy this choice was.
Mack possessed many estimable qualities, but he should
never have been raised to the post of supreme command.   His intelligence, industry, and perseverance
fitted him for the place of Quartermaster-General:
the task of commanding an army was beyond his
powers.

At the approach of a war, in the preparation of
which Napoleon had put forth all his strength, the
ties between the Courts of Vienna and St. Petersburg,
which the issue of the campaign of 1799 and the extra-
vagances of Paul I. had greatly loosened, were drawn
closer.

It was at the end of the year 1804 that I received
the first communication respecting this great undertaking, in which the two courts were excessively anxious
to gain the concurrence of Prussia.   It was my task
to smooth the way for this accession.

This seemed to me difficult, on account of the
known sentiments of the men at that time entrusted
with the direction of Prussian policy.   The more
decidedly the parties in Berlin were opposed to each
other, the more difficult was it to make them see their
true interests.   The Emperor sent his brother the
Archduke Antony to Berlin.   His presence had no
result.   He returned to Vienna, leaving things as he
found them.   The Emperor Alexander then sent Prince
Dolgoruki, one of the younger advisers whom he had
gathered round him since he mounted the throne, a
man full of fire and spirit, but of a nature nowise fitted
for such a critical mission.   As he had been instructed

by his master to adhere to me in everything, I could influence his conduct, but not direct it. The Russian ambassador in Berlin, Herr von Alopäus, had filled that position for many years; his relations with the most influential persons in the government were most confidential; and yet the Emperor Alexander had no faith in his energy. I was therefore requested by that monarch to supply the deficiencies of his minister.

At last the Emperor Alexander, tired out by the continued evasiveness of the language used by the Prussian cabinet, decided on a most dangerous step. He would, in fact, force the King of Prussia to a decision, and at the same time weaken his strength by pushing on his own army to the frontier of East Prussia, where he halted. This military movement was intended to support the negotiations which were being carried on by the representatives of Russia and Austria. But the object was not attained; the threat, on the contrary, rather increased the opposition. Under the influence of his different advisers, the King became more and more vacillating, and could not come to any resolution. Then there followed an interchange of letters between the two monarchs, which led to no definite result, and the Emperor Alexander, whose impatience increased daily, was more and more inclined to take violent measures. I remember a singular circumstance which occurred at this time, which I will not omit to mention.

I received the news one day that the Emperor Alexander was to strike a heavy blow. At a given hour a courier was to reach Herr von Alopäus with a communication to the King of Prussia to announce that the Russian army, without further delay, was to cross the frontier. The actual entry of the troops was to take place simultaneously with the arrival of the notice. When I received this news, I found that the warning had come too late; if I could have done so, I would have addressed to the Emperor Alexander the most urgent request that he would abstain from a course which certainly must end in throwing Prussia into the arms of France. It was on the eve of the catastrophe at Ulm when the Austrian forces were pushing on by forced marches to this point. Nothing promised success to the ill-considered step of the Emperor Alexander, especially if the character of Frederick William III. were considered. I could do nothing but await the event.

The Russian courier was to arrive in the evening. At nine o'clock I went to the ambassador, who was detained at home by a slight indisposition. Under the most frivolous pretexts, I remained with him till nearly midnight; then the sound of a carriage, which stopped at the door of his hotel, told me that the moment of the crisis had come. The arrival of a courier from the Russian head-quarters was announced. Herr von Alopäus had the despatches brought to him, and immediately began to open them. We stood close to a desk, at which the aged ambassador was accustomed to stand and write.

In spite of his increasing years Herr von Alopäus was vivacious almost to the point of impetuosity. In placing the rather bulky despatches on the writing-desk some papers fell on the floor, which we picked up. Beside the folio sheets which dropped I had remarked distinctly a letter of small size, and in fact, from the other despatches this was seen to be a letter in the Emperor's own hand to the King of Prussia, of which a copy was enclosed. In this letter his Majesty informed

the King that he had ordered his army to cross the
Prussian frontier.   The contents of these despatches
threw Herr von Alopäus into the greatest excitement ;
it would have had the same effect upon me, if I had
not been prepared beforehand.   He went off into very
just remarks on the danger of the situation, and said
at last : ' The die is cast ! nothing more remains to me
but to do the bidding of the Emperor, and hand over
the letter of his Imperial Majesty to the King.'

But the letter had vanished.   In his sudden fright
at not finding it, and thinking of the gravity of the
complication which must arise from the non-execution
of the orders he had received, Herr von Alopäus
tried to ascribe the absence of the autograph itself
to an act of forgetfulness in the sender.   As for me,
I certainly saw a sealed letter with my own eyes,
and now it was not there !   For more than half an
hour we sought under all the furniture without finding it ; Alopäus in an impulse of despair clasped his
head with both hands, and at this moment the Emperor's letter fell to the floor ; it had got into a fold
in the sleeve of his dressing-gown !

The Russians, however, did not cross the frontier then,
as was intended.   The Emperor Alexander thought
better of it, and an attempt was made to overcome
the vacillation of the King by a meeting of the two
monarchs, at which the Emperor might influence him
personally.

Our negotiations had taken this new phase, when
Prince Dolgoruki was commissioned to deliver to the
King another letter from the Emperor, in which he
invited the King to the meeting already arranged, and
repeated the threat of sending his troops through Prus
sian territory.   Herr von Alopäus wrote to the minister

asking an audience, with the urgent request that, consi-
dering the gravity of the case, Prince Dolgoruki and he
should be admitted to the King, who was residing at
Potsdam, as quickly as possible.

The same day Dolgoruki came to me. We agreed
as to the language which he should hold with the King,
while I assured him of my best support. 'I fear, however,' said I to him as we parted, ' that the consequence
of this pressure will be the alliance of Prussia with
France.' The prince promised to inform me, immediately on his return from Potsdam, of all that had
taken place.

Prince Dolgoruki and Herr von Alopäus came to
me on October 6, and told me what had occurred.
They had on that day handed to the King the Emperor's letter. His Majesty read it, and declared without waiting a moment that he had offered the neutrality
of Prussia to the belligerent powers, and that the
moment one of those powers by violating his territory
broke that neutrality, he considered himself at war
with them. 'Return to the Emperor, gentlemen,' continued the King, 'and inform him of my unalterable
decision. 'I will write him a letter to the same effect.'
With this he dismissed the two ambassadors.

Hardly, however, had they left Potsdam than Baron
Hardenberg, who happened to be at the palace, was
sent after them to Berlin, to summon them back to the
King. His Majesty had just received the news that
Napoleon had invaded the neutral Prussian territory at Anspach, in order to outflank the Austrian
army concentrated at Ulm. The King said to his minister : 'Matters have taken another turn ; go at once
to Prince Dolgoruki. He will take with him a letter,
in which I will inform the Emperor that the frontiers of

my kingdom are open to him.' Never, perhaps, have such important events come together in one decisive moment.

The King of Prussia's letter to the Emperor of Russia was taken to him by Prince Dolgoruki, and the King invited me to come to him at Potsdam.

I had a long conversation with the King, which confirmed me in my view of the danger of the steps taken by the Emperor Alexander in such grave circumstances. This prince, vehement and full of energy, impulsive, always in danger of acting rashly, and viewing things from the standpoint of his pet ideas, had on coming to the throne surrounded himself with a council formed of persons of his own age, whom he honoured with the name of friends. Among these were Prince Adam Czartoryski and Prince Dolgoruki. The former managed the affairs of the Foreign Office; the latter was one of those general officers of whom his Majesty constantly took counsel. As I have said, he was gifted with a warm imagination, and influenced the Emperor more than any one else with the idea of binding the hands of the King Frederick William—an enterprise which, from the character of that prince, must necessarily fail. The attitude of the King of Prussia was founded on strict neutrality, and in this he acted in good faith. The violent measures of Napoleon and Alexander, similar in character and coincident in time, left the King only the choice which of two insults he should resent; he chose without hesitation to pass by that which in form was the least injurious. Alexander had made known to the King, in a manner as peremptory as unusual, his determination to violate the neutrality of Prussia. Napoleon, on the contrary, admitted the neutrality of this power, and yet violated it. The King felt Napoleon's proceeding to be the more bitter insult.

Immediately after Alexander had received the King's letter, sent by Prince Dolgoruki, he set out on the road to Potsdam. The King invited the reigning Duke of Brunswick to come at once and begin the negotiations for the entry of Prussia into alliance with the two Imperial courts. This negotiation was conducted, on the one hand, by the Emperor Alexander and myself; on the Prussian side by Count Haugwitz for the political part, and by the Duke of Brunswick, to whom the King had given the command of the army, for the military part. Prince Adam Czartoryski, then Minister for Foreign Affairs of the Emperor of Russia, was the official representative of the Emperor; but in reality, the Emperor himself conducted the negotiations. My relations with his Imperial Majesty date from this epoch, and they afterwards became most confidential.

From the first moment, the Emperor and I fell under the ill-will of the Prussian negotiators. With ill-concealed anger, they resorted to every imaginable pretext to protract the arrangements which, in face of the calamitous circumstances of the war on the Danube, grew more and more urgent. Certainly these events were of a kind to make the Prussian Cabinet thoughtful. Yet of all resolutions they took the very worst. When the breach with France took place, the King should either have again proclaimed his neutrality, at the risk of seeing it violated a second time by one or other of the belligerent powers, or he should, with the least possible delay, have joined his forces with the Allies, and have endeavoured by energetic action to restore the chances of war in their favour and his own. A calculation so simple did not enter the head of Count Haugwitz, and it found no response in the irresolute character of the Duke of Brunswick. The two Prussian negotiators made the worst possible choice, they decided for a system of vacillation.

At last the King made up his mind. A treaty of alliance between the three courts was signed at Potsdam on November 5, and the Emperor Alexander went immediately to the head-quarters of the Emperor Francis.

Count Haugwitz, who could not evade the completion of the treaty of alliance, left open a backdoor of escape. He caused the King to send him to Napoleon to inform him, on the part of the King, that the King had decided to unite his forces with those of the two Imperial courts, in case the French army should not halt in its victorious career. The days necessary to carry out this step were duly calculated. At his departure, the Czar had given me full powers, and in his name also I was to watch over the strict fulfilment of the engagements just made. Without loss of time the Prussian army marched towards the Upper Danube.

Just at this time the war of 1805 entered its last phase. Count Haugwitz, having delayed his departure from Berlin more than eight days beyond the time agreed upon, did not find Napoleon at Vienna, and went to join him at Brünn. But, instead of executing his commission, he gave it the character of a simple act of politeness on the part of the King his master. Napoleon sent him back to Vienna. He was preparing to offer battle, to which the Emperor Alexander also was pressing forward. Napoleon found himself in a very dangerous position. The Archduke Charles was advancing by forced marches with the army of Italy through Styria; the Prussian army was in movement towards Regensburg; and, lastly, the news from Paris of the internal condition of France was of the most disquieting cha-

racter. If the allied armies, instead of offering battle
at Austerlitz, had halted at a suitable distance, the French
army would have been forced to fall back upon Vienna,
and the Allies would then have been able again to take
the offensive with vigour. Tyrol and even Upper
Austria only waited for this to rise in one mass. Thus
the chances of war were all in favour of the Allies,
and never was position more grave than that of Napoleon. The Emperor Francis himself tried every argument to dissuade the Emperor Alexander from offering
battle. It was, however, begun, and its results lie before
us in the Peace of Pressburg.

The Emperor bestowed on me the order of the grand
cross of St. Stephen, in recognition of the services which
he condescended to see in my share in the conclusion
of the league with Prussia. This league was, thanks
to the attitude of Count Haugwitz, a fruitless one.
When he presented himself to the Emperor Napoleon
after his entrance into Vienna, and offered him his
congratulations on the victory, Napoleon asked him
whether if the event had been different he would have
spoken to him of the friendship of the King his master.
Count Haugwitz took no notice of the sarcasm, and negotiated for the union of the Electorate of Hanover
with Prussia. Napoleon gave, in fact, his consent to
this, for, aiming as he did at the destruction of Germany, nothing could better serve his plans than a union
of that character, which was a direct attack on the
existence of the German Empire, and at the same time
concealed within itself the germ of an irreparable
breach between Prussia and Great Britain.

Vienna was the theatre of all these not very honourable arrangements, which Count Haugwitz concealed
from the King his master till his return to Berlin.

This return he delayed as long as possible, sometimes
on the plea of health, sometimes pretending important
business which he carefully kept under a veil of mys-
tery. At last he made his appearance at Potsdam,
and gave the King an account of his political industry,
leaving to the King the choice between the ratification
of the act concluded by Haugwitz *sub spe rati*, and the
deposition of the negotiator. The King ratified the
treaty, but dismissed Count Haugwitz from his office,
which he conferred on Freiherr von Hardenberg.

Napoleon in imperial robes.

CHAPTER IV.

AS AUSTRIAN AMBASSADOR AT THE COURT OF NAPOLEON.

(1806—1809.)

Retirement of Colloredo and Cobenzl—Stadion appointed Minister for
Foreign Affairs—Metternich appointed to St. Petersburg: goes, instead,
to Paris—Reasons for this change—Conversation with the Emperor
Francis—Little instruction from the Archives—Journey from Vienna—
Detention in Strasburg—Arrival in Paris—Beginning of public life
there—With Talleyrand—First audience of Napoleon in St.-Cloud—
Jena, the summit of Napoleon's power—The mistakes of Prussia—Napoleon's mistakes—Bulletins—The *gloire nationale*—Napoleon's return from
the banks of the Niemen (Memel)—Dalberg's audience on taking leave—
Count Tolskoy—Count Nesselrode—Napoleon glances towards Spain—
Meeting of the monarchs at Erfurt—Count Romanzow—Metternich's
passive attitude—Lafayette—Barrère—The great audience of August 15,
1808—Champagny silenced—Arrival at Vienna—The Austrian position
—Conversation with the Emperor Francis—Metternich's views on the
war—Napoleon's attitude—Diplomatic relations with Austria broken off
—Metternich's departure prevented, and the reason for this—The internal
condition of France—Wealth of the French marshals—Napoleon's
position—Anti-warlike disposition of the great office-bearers and marshals of France—Characteristics of Talleyrand, Fouché, and Cambacérès
—Metternich's departure from Paris as prisoner under escort—Report of
the battle of Aspern—Visit to the Empress Josephine at Strasburg—
Arrival at Vienna—Metternich's father, with the Archbishop of Vienna,
Count Pergen, and Hardegg, appointed to Geiseln—Conversation with
Champagny—Interned in the Villa of Grünberg—General Savary's visit
—Departure for the place of exchange—Contrary orders—Napoleon's excuses—Night-quarters in Acs—An Austrian battery fires at Metternich's
carriage—Return to Raab—Exchanged at last—Colonel Avy—Reception by the Emperor Francis—Stadion's appointment—Preparation for
battle—Retreat of the Austrian army—Head-quarters in Znaim.

THE consequences of the battle of Austerlitz made it
impossible for those men who had undertaken the war of
1805 to remain in office. Count Colloredo, the cabinet

minister, and Count Cobenzl, the Vice-Chancellor of
Courland State, resigned, and the Emperor appointed
Count Stadion, his ambassador at St. Petersburg, to be
Minister of Foreign Affairs. As the Emperor Alexander
had wished me to be ambassador there, I was ordered
to leave Berlin, and to repair to my new appointment, by
way of Vienna. At the beginning of April I reached
that city, and presented myself to Count Stadion, who
informed me that not St. Petersburg, but Paris, was to
be my destination. Count Philip Cobenzl, who had
been selected for the embassy in France, had been objected to by Napoleon, who pointed out me as the
representative of Austria most suitable to strengthen
those relations he was now anxious to see established
between the two Empires.

I afterwards learned that the reasons which actuated
Napoleon on this occasion were the following:—My
French colleague in Berlin was M. de Laforest, before
mentioned, a confidant of Prince Talleyrand. At the
moment of extreme tension, just before the conclusion
of the alliance between Austria, Russia and Prussia, the
position of M. de Laforest had become most difficult. It
had, however, always been my habit not to mingle business affairs with personal matters, and so I endeavoured
to maintain relations with my French colleague on a
footing of frank courtesy. These relations continued
during all the different phases of the affair. This did
not escape the notice of Talleyrand, whose policy was
not averse to the establishment of good relations between France and Austria. The influence of Count
Philip Cobenzl had become stale in Paris, a new man
was wanted there : the choice fell on me.

This change in my destination, when I learned it,
fell upon me like a thunder-bolt. I resigned the posi-

tion at St. Petersburg, with reluctance, for the personal relations in which I stood to the Emperor Alexander allowed me to hope that I might render service there to my monarch, and at the same time count on a sphere of action more suited to my views than that which awaited me in Paris, face to face with Napoleon.   The task of representing Austria in France, immediately after the Peace of Pressburg, presented so many difficulties, that I feared I should not be adequate to them. The next day I waited on the Emperor Francis, and ventured to describe the embarrassment of my position. He received me with his usual kindness, praised me for my conduct in Berlin, and set before me the necessity of accommodating myself to what he called my destiny, with expressions which made it impossible for me to oppose his wishes.

I was thus placed in a position opposed to my inclinations, but being determined always to subordinate them to a feeling of duty, I endeavoured to make clear to myself the line I ought to take. Napoleon seemed to me the incarnation of the Revolution ; while in the Austrian Power which I had to represent at his court, I saw the surest guardian of the principles which alone guaranteed general peace and political equilibrium.   When I looked at my task from this point of view, the great importance of the functions I had to perform rose before me.   I did not, indeed, fear to go wrong, as so many had done, from a heated imagination or self-love, for I felt myself free from these failings ; but, on the other hand, I knew the many and dangerous rocks in my new position, and I resolved for the present, to keep my ambition within very modest bounds, and at least to prevent evil when I saw the impossibility of doing good.

I searched in the archives of the chancellery, but

found little to help me. The French Revolution was not yet understood by the men whom fate had called on, to deal with this monstrous social catastrophe. The rapidity of the career of Napoleon had dazzled many spectators, and left them little time to weigh, impartially and quietly, the conditions on which his existence rested. I addressed myself to this task with pleasure, convinced as I was that the analysis of this personified product of the Revolution must necessarily explain to me how this man, from so mean a starting-point, could have raised himself to such a height. Some saw in Napoleon only the great general; some saw the ground of his elevation in his political talents; while others regarded him merely as an adventurer favoured by fortune : all forgot that for the explanation of the astonishing success of this man, it was indispensable to connect his personal qualities with the circumstances in which he lived.

I left Vienna in July 1806. When I arrived in Strasburg, I was not allowed to continue my journey; the order had been given in Paris, but the pretext made use of by the local authorities was, that they could not allow me to continue my journey without a positive order. The true cause of this unjustifiable proceeding was, however, the presence of Herr Oubril in Paris, through whose assistance Napoleon hoped to arrive at an understanding with the Russian court. Till this understanding, to which the Emperor Alexander afterwards refused his consent, was arrived at, the Emperor of the French seemed not to wish for my presence in Paris. If, indeed, I had been there, I should have used my influence to prevent that young and inexperienced negotiator from compromising himself in so painful a manner. When the negotiations with Herr Oubril

had once been concluded *sub spe rati*, I was allowed to
continue my journey to Paris, where I arrived on August
4. The next day I went to the Prince of Benevento
(Talleyrand), then Minister for Foreign Affairs, whom I
did not as yet personally know. He received me with
the greatest cordiality, showed himself inclined to closer
relations between France and Austria, and boasted of
the moderation which he had displayed during the
negotiations of the Peace of Pressburg. As this assertion
was well founded, I took up my own position, and explained to him what the Emperor understood by friendly
relations, which must not be confounded with submission.

This was, in fact, the beginning of my public life.
All that had gone before might have shown the independence of my character. As a man of principles,
I could not and I would not bend when it came to the
point of defending them. Within a short space of time
destiny had placed me face to face with the man who at
this epoch ruled the affairs of the world ; I felt it my
duty and I had the courage never to offer to mere circumstance a sacrifice which I could not defend to my
conscience both as a statesman and as a private individual. This voice of conscience I followed ; and I
do not think it was a good inspiration of Napoleon's,
which called me to functions which gave me the opportunity of appreciating his excellences, but also the
possibility of discovering the faults which at last led him
to ruin and freed Europe from the oppression under
which it languished.

This study put means into my hand, the efficacy
of which I had the opportunity of proving in a few
years.

I presented myself to Napoleon, without delivering

an address at the first audience I had at St.-Cloud, as was the custom of my colleagues. I confined myself to stating that as, in accordance with his own wishes, I had been chosen to represent the Emperor of Austria at his court, I should strive on every occasion to strengthen the good relations between the two empires on that basis upon which alone a lasting peace could be established between independent states. Napoleon answered me in the same simple style, and our subsequent personal relations took their tone from this first meeting.

France at that time felt the need of order, and would easily have been led in that direction, if Napoleon's love of conquest had not forced it to a system which ultimately led him to his ruin. War with Prussia was imminent : yet Napoleon might have acted so as to avoid it. This he would not do ; and the consequences would have justified the choice made by Napoleon, had he not abused the victory.

In this Autobiography there will not be found a narrative of events belonging to diplomatic and military history ; materials for the history of the time must be drawn from the state archives of official correspondence. It does not belong to the plan I set before me to specify the mass of labours which in the long course of my public life I was able to achieve. The present work is intended only to communicate what concerns myself, or has reference to the tone of mind which the circumstances of my time have produced in me, those of which I was a mere spectator and those in which I have myself played a part.

According to my opinion, Napoleon reached the summit of his power in the victory of Jena. If, instead of the destruction of Prussia, he had limited his ambition to the weakening of that power, and had then annexed it to the Confederation of the Rhine, the enormous edifice which he had succeeded in erecting would have gained a foundation of strength and solidity, which the Peace of Tilsit did not gain for it; indeed, the conditions of that peace were so hard and over-strained that it essentially contributed to its downfall.

The mistake which the Prussians made in 1805 in not uniting their strength with that of Austria and Russia, was renewed in the rising of 1806; and yet it was to this repeated mistake, that we owe the libera-tion of Europe from the yoke which Napoleon's love of conquest had imposed upon it. For King Frederick William III. the war of 1806 was not premeditated, but rather the effect of an agitation which he had not the strength to resist. Prince Louis Ferdinand and the feeble *élite* of the army were at the head of the agitation for war. The great mass of the army as well as of the people were under the spell of the neutrality which the King contrived to maintain after the Peace of Basle, and which, after the dissolution of the German Em-pire, had given Prussia a kind of protectorate over North Germany. This position was weak on the face of it, and although it flattered the short-sighted plans of such men as Count Haugwitz, Lombard, and General von Pfuel, it hindered everything like enthusiasm in the nation. When Napoleon, in 1805, in order to ensure the success of a strategic combination, ventured to violate the neutral Prussian territory, he showed how well he understood the condition of Prussia; and cer-tainly the attitude of Count Haugwitz after the battle of Austerlitz was not calculated to give him a different impression of the energy of that power. I am con-vinced, therefore, that the political mistake committed by Napoleon, after his enormous successes during the whole campaign, was chiefly the consequence of the false idea he had formed of the thorough exhaustion of the Prussian power. When Napoleon had reduced this kingdom to the condition of the Peace of Tilsit, he believed that he could leave it to die a natural death ; and in his opinion the kingdoms of Westphalia and Saxony were the natural heirs of Prussia.

I took leave in the year 1810 to draw Napoleon's attention to what I thought a mistake in his calculation. He did not contradict me, and added, 'I had taken it in hand, and must finish the work I had begun. You see, too, what Prussia is good for.' The events of a few years later than this prove that Napoleon was not infallible in his calculations : they justified mine.

There are few chapters in the history of nations which exhibit such astonishing vicissitudes of fortune as the history of Prussia from the death of the great Frederick till the Peace of Tilsit. Rising in the course of four reigns from the position of an electorate to a power of the first rank, this monarchy, after the campaigns of 1806 and 1807, was shaken to its very foundations. All seems contradiction in the annals of Prussia, and these annals comprise scarcely one century. In less than this period a barren and thinly populated country rose to a height of power which assigned to its rulers more than once the part of umpires in Europe, and this height of power it reached amid storms and agitations which threatened it at home and abroad. From the year 1740 there was not a moment when the Prussian army was not in active service. Its standing army, though out of all proportion to the number of the people, or the resources of the country, far from exhausting

these, on the contrary, raised the monarchy to a height
of power not aspired to in the wildest dreams of its
greatest princes.   Frederick II. on his deathbed said
to his young nephew that his successors would do
more than he had done if they knew how to maintain
his conquests.   But, in fact, they doubled them.   And
this state did not grow and increase in the midst of less
civilised nations.   On the contrary, all its conquests were
over those which surpassed it in wealth and power.
The Revolution, which since 1789 threatened to engulf
the civilised world, contributed to the aggrandisement
of Prussia.   All the Powers that went to war with
France exhausted themselves.   Prussia alone drew advantage from all circumstances ; and when she found
herself with other states put down for the time, she
went her own way with quiet steps and accommodated
herself to the conqueror.   Every campaign gave her
a pretext for extending her influence ; every truce either
confirmed an encroachment on a weak and timid
neighbour, or contrived that such should voluntarily
place itself under her banner ; lastly, every peace
brought her a reward for exertions which she had
nevertheless made only to serve her own purposes.
Such were the consequences of the mighty impulse
given to the country by the genius of her first kings.

The observations which my position in the French
capital enabled me to make during the whole duration
of the war of 1806 and 1807 were in absolute contradiction to the reports industriously circulated by the
organs of the Government on the condition of the
country.   I had the opportunity of convincing myself
of the extreme care taken by the Emperor to magnify
the effect of his victories.   The account of some previous victory was spread through Paris previous to the

officially prepared news of a defeat; the members of
the Government itself might act as if in the greatest
anxiety, whilst the cannon of the Invalides thundered
forth the news of a victory already known.

Napoleon, in making use of such petty means, had
doubtless the double object of adding brilliancy to his
successes, and of furnishing the means to his police of
ascertaining the feelings of individuals.   With respect to
the first, he may have succeeded to a certain point, but
not in regard to the latter.   A stupor then reigned in
Paris, produced by a sense of the weight which the Emperor had laid upon all classes of society.   With the exception of *agents provocateurs*, no person of any influence
would have ventured to express aloud any sentiment
unpleasant to the Government; but after all the loud
talkers are not really the persons to be feared.   The impression made on the public of Paris by the news of
a battle won by Napoleon was certainly not that of joy:
it was satisfaction that France had escaped the consequences, and at seeing that her internal peace was not
endangered.   The Emperor might with good right say at
that time *La France c'est moi!*   The revolutionary
elements were only smothered.   The country had not
one friend in Europe, and an immeasurable feeling of
unrest reigned amid the rejoicings for a victory of the
French army, for everyone knew that these victories
made new ones necessary to complete the work, the
ultimate extent of which no one could foresee.   The
phrase *gloire nationale*, which in the Restoration acted
like magic, had not then the same effect.   With a few
exceptions, the nation would willingly have exchanged
glory for safety.   Under the Restoration the appeal to
la gloire was a weapon of the Bonapartist and revolutionary opposition; under the Empire the opposition

was unanimous in its repudiation of a warlike tendency.

Intoxicated with victory, Napoleon returned from the banks of the Niemen to Paris. The first impression of the unrestrained idea of power of the insatiable conqueror was given to the diplomatic corps at the customary reception, when all the assembled representatives of foreign powers had in turn to hear the unpleasant things from the mouth of the Emperor. Sarcasm of every kind was interspersed with warlike menaces. I came off the best, although in the negotiations on the adjustment of the boundary between Austria and the kingdom of Italy, which at that time came to a conclusion in the Convention of Fontainebleau, the feeling of Napoleon betrayed itself in a way anything but satisfactory to the wishes of Austria.

It was at this time that the Princes of the new Confederation of the Rhine came to Paris, to do homage to their new master and to congratulate him on his fresh victories. At their head was the Prince Primate Freiherr von Dalberg. Six weeks after the arrival of that Prince, I happened to have an audience of Napoleon at St.-Cloud. In the ante-room I met the Prince Primate, who had come to take leave of the Emperor. He was just speaking to me of the grand prospects of the Bund, of the thankfulness of all its members to the Emperor Napoleon, and of the high destiny to which the German Fatherland was called, when he was invited to enter the Emperor's closet. He remained about eight or ten minutes with the Emperor, then came my turn.

Napoleon excused himself that he had kept me waiting so long. I remarked that to me at least the time had passed quickly, that the audience of the Prince Primate had not seemed to me to be a long one;

at any rate for a farewell audience. 'Well, what would you have?' said Napoleon smiling: 'this man is full of empty dreams. He torments me continually to arrange the constitution of what he calls the German Fatherland. He wants his Regensburg, his Imperial court of supreme judicature with all the traditions of the old German Empire. He tried to speak again of these absurdities, but I cut him short. "Monsieur l'Abbé," I said to him, "I will tell you my secret. In Germany the small people want to be protected against the great people; the great wish to govern according to their own fancy; now, as I only want from the federation men and money, and as it is the great people and not the small who can provide me with both, I leave the former alone in peace, and the second have only to settle themselves as best they may!"'

My personal relations with Napoleon soon assumed the same character which they had before he took the field. About that time General Count Peter Tolstoy arrived in France as ambassador from Russia. The Emperor Alexander had enjoined him to attach himself to me, and to follow my advice. Count Tolstoy had not before served in the diplomatic line, and from the turn of his mind and his exclusively military knowledge he never was successful in this career; and in accepting the post of Ambassador in Paris he merely submitted to the will of the Emperor. The choice of the Emperor Alexander was, in my opinion, well suited to the position of affairs. As a zealous conservative, by nature and experience, the enemy of the system of conquest, this 'Ambassador against his will' made no secret of his inclinations, and thereby gained the respect of men whose tendencies he had been directed to observe. Count Nesselrode, afterwards Vice-Chancellor of the

Russian Empire, filled the post of first Secretary of Legation under Count Tolstoy, and from this time date the relations of personal confidence between us which have been maintained through the varied phases of our public life.

After the Peace of Tilsit, the Emperor of the French turned his eyes on Spain.   In order to secure the carrying out of his plans, he thought it necessary to cripple Russia, after conquering Austria and Prussia, in two successive wars, and covering the eastern frontier of his Empire by the Confederation of the Rhine.   The undertaking had but too great success at Erfurt.   The conference which took place there between Napoleon and Alexander was a snare for the Russian monarch. In reality, Napoleon's thoughts were directed neither against Turkey nor against Asia ; and if the hatred which he entertained for England led him to think for a moment of attacking her in her Indian possessions, this project existed only as an eventuality, dependent on the concurrence of circumstances as yet remote. Napoleon occupied himself rather with perfecting his Continental system, and with the expulsion of the Bourbons from the throne of Spain.   The extravagance of these gigantic schemes brought about the fall of Napoleon a few years later, and the expedition against Spain, which beyond any doubt was a thoroughly mistaken idea on his part, only accelerated the catastrophe.

Napoleon left Paris in August.   History has undertaken to describe the events of which Spain was the theatre, and to record for posterity the reaction of those events on the destiny of Europe.   They made a most lively impression upon the Austrian Cabinet; and I felt them the more, from my knowledge of them in my official capacity.   Desirous of leaving a position where

I could not obtain the necessary information, I asked leave, during the absence of the Emperor from Paris, to go to Vienna in order to give them the news I possessed, and learn some for myself. Leave being granted to me, I started on October 4, and arrived in Vienna on the 10th.

The meeting of the monarchs took place at Erfurt in September and October, 1808. Thither General Baron Vincent was sent from Vienna, under the pretext of welcoming the two Emperors; he had acted as ambassador in Paris from the peace of 1805 till my arrival. His candid and loyal character, as well as the tendency of his mind, had won Napoleon's regard. The Emperor Francis could not have made a better choice for so critical a mission. Through him and my colleague Tolstoy, I was kept informed of what passed at Erfurt, and could not but foresee, that enormous complications were inevitable from the approach of two such great potentates as Napoleon and Alexander—an approach which had no real basis, and was only a trap laid for the Russian monarch on the part of the French Emperor. But the calculation was wrong, because Napoleon, when he speculated on deluding the Emperor of Russia for a time, was quite mistaken as to the time necessary for accomplishing the overthrow of Spain.

The Chancellor, Count Romanzow, followed Napoleon to Paris, after his return from Erfurt, as closely as possible. Romanzow knew me from my earliest youth, for when he resided at Frankfort as Russian Ambassador to the Rhenish Courts, he was a colleague of my father. During his residence at Paris, Count Romanzow was extremely intimate with me, and anxiously endeavoured to flatter the new ally of Russia. All that

Count Romanzow did was in good faith, and I doubt
not that he took this alliance to be quite sincere. I
am sure that he only followed the guidance of his conscience, when he endeavoured to correct my ideas with
regard to this new political phase. Count Romanzow,
a clever man, though of no deep intellect, was caught
in the nets which Napoleon spread for him. Loaded by
Napoleon with favours, he took all these attentions as
genuine, and was at last so dazzled by them that in the
course of a long conversation, I do not now remember
on what subject, he thought to silence me with the following words : 'I have Napoleon in my pocket ; do you
think that I am going to let him go ?' By a curious
coincidence, it happened that I had just come from the
Emperor, and my conversation with him had given me
an impression which scarcely agreed with this. Napoleon had, in fact, spoken to me of the Chancellor with
extreme candour, and made no secret of his mean
opinion of him as a statesman.

My position was a peculiar one. I was placed at
the most prominent post for observing the movement
of which the Emperor of the French was the centre.
I represented at his court a great monarch, whose
kingdom had yielded under the force of circumstances,
but which was ready to rise on the first opportunity.
I was penetrated with the feeling of danger to my
country, if it entered on a new war with France without having more probable chances of success ; and I
conceived that my task consisted in playing the part
of a quiet and impartial spectator—impartial, so far
as this might be possible to a man of feeling, at an
epoch when the world was passing through a social
transformation. Nowhere was the conflict between the
fermenting elements more vehement than in the great

country in which I was living. Beyond the confines of France, Governments had no other care than to withstand the political encroachments of the conqueror who had placed the Imperial crown on his head. The conflict between the different systems of government really existed only in France. Raised by the Revolution to the summit of power, Napoleon endeavoured to prop up by monarchical institutions the throne he had made for himself. The destructive parties, having to do with a man equally great as a statesman and as a general, who knew his country and the spirit of the nation better than any who ever guided the destinies of France, were above all anxious to save from the wreck of their works all they could secure from the encroachments of the Imperial power. These efforts were impotent; but they were not the less worthy of observation.

My impartial attitude gained me the confidence of the most prominent men of different parties, beginning with Napoleon himself. One individual I must except. I never saw Lafayette. When the Emperor spoke to me of him, he did so with an expression of that contempt which he had for everyone whom he considered an *idéologue*. Among the most eager courtiers of the Empire might be seen the fiercest partisans of a Government which, after it had shed blood in streams, vanished like smoke under the Directory. Napoleon spoke of these men with the deepest scorn; he said to me one day: 'These people were the perpetrators of impious deeds but a short time ago; now I use them in building up my new social edifice. There are some good workmen among them; the mischief is, that they all want to be architects. That is always the case with the French; there is hardly one among them who does not think himself capable of governing the country!'

Among the dismal celebrities of a bloody epoch I will mention Barère, who gained the nickname of the Anacreon of the Guillotine. To my great surprise, this man one day desired an interview with me. I found in him the traces of that spurious refinement which was also a characteristic of Robespierre. The reason of his coming was to ask a favour for one of his relations. To judge from his physiognomy, one might have taken him for the most harmless creature in the world. I shall perhaps have to speak again of persons of the same stamp as Barère and Merlin de Thionville, whose reign ended with the Reign of Terror.

Napoleon's mind was full, as I have said before, of the overthrow of Spain. He was preparing to appear personally on the scene where the great drama was to be played. This might lead to contingencies for which the Vienna Cabinet must provide. The preparations made in Austria pointed to warlike designs. Before he left Paris, Napoleon, wishing to insult Austria, chose for the purpose the ceremonious audience which he was accustomed to grant to the diplomatic body on his *fête*, August 15.*

These audiences took place immediately before the service, which the Emperor, accompanied by a great retinue, attended in the chapel at St.-Cloud. Just before noon the diplomatic corps was conducted to the audience-chamber. I took my usual place in the circle, having Count Tolstoy on my right, the rest of the diplomatic

* Till the Concordat, no day had been set apart in the calendar for Saint Napoleon. The Emperor of the French obtained the permission of Pope Pius VII., however, to have his festival on the day of the Assumption of the Virgin. As this day was kept as a great festival in consequence of the reconciliation with the Roman Court, the Emperor chose it in order that his *fête* might coincide with a religious festival observed throughout France.

corps being arranged in a semicircle, in the centre of which was the Emperor. At such ceremonials the princes of his family were ranged behind him, then the cabinet ministers, the members of the court, and the adjutants.

After some minutes of unusual silence, Napoleon advanced towards me with great solemnity. He stopped two feet in front of me, and addressed me in a loud voice and pompous tone: ' Well, Sir Ambassador, what does the Emperor, your master, want—does he intend to call me back to Vienna?' This address did not disconcert me; I answered him calmly, and in no less elevated tones. Our conversation the longer it lasted took on Napoleon's side more and more the character of a public manifestation, Napoleon raising his voice as he always did, when he had the double end in view of intimidating the person he was addressing and of making an effect on the rest of his hearers. I did not alter my tone, and met his worthless arguments with the weapon of irony; from time to time Napoleon appealed to Count Tolstoy as a witness; but when he observed that the Count preserved an unbroken silence, he turned round, breaking off in the midst of a sentence, and strode to the chapel without completing the round of the circle. This scene lasted more than half an hour. The Empress Josephine and her train waited in the hall through which the Emperor had to pass, and no one could explain the reason of the length of this so-called diplomatic audience.

As soon as Napoleon had left the audience-chamber, all my colleagues thronged round me, to congratulate me on having, as they said, given the Emperor a lesson. A few hours afterwards I went to the Hôtel of Count Champagny, then Minister of Foreign Affairs, who gave a great banquet in honour of the day. On my entrance he said to me, he was ordered by his master, the Emperor, to assure me, that the scene at the audience had nothing personal in it; and that his master's intention had merely been to explain the position. I assured the minister that I too put the same construction on the incident; and, for my part, did not regret that the Emperor had given me the opportunity to explain before assembled Europe what the monarch whom I had the honour to represent wished—and what he did not wish. 'Europe,' I continued, 'will be able to judge on which side reason and right are to be found.' Count Champagny made no answer.

In order to understand the moral view by which the Austrian cabinet was actuated, it will be enough to refer to the political relations existing in Europe. Under the weight of the unhappy issue of the war of 1805, Austria had collapsed. The Confederation of the Rhine, under the protection of the French Emperor, had taken the place of the German Empire; and after the last war between France and Prussia the Princes of North Germany also had entered this Confederation. Tyrol had joined Bavaria, and the dukedom of Warsaw, under the supremacy of the King of Saxony, was pushed in between Austria and Russia. The Peace of Tilsit had destroyed the Prussian power, and from the conference of Erfurt there had resulted an illusive alliance between Russia and France, the twofold object of which was the silent assent of the former power to the attacks of the latter, and the partition of the Ottoman Empire between the two, adjusted on the supposition of its impending fall.

Austria, therefore, was in a position in which she could not possibly maintain herself. The Imperial cabinet was not alone in this feeling. Napoleon was so

convinced of it that he looked upon Austria as a prize
in prospect for one of his new German allies.   Not only
then was a renewal of the war in the nature of things,
but it was for our Empire an absolute condition of its
existence.   This question was to my mind settled.   But
the points which remained, and, in my view, required
ripe consideration, were, the choice of the right moment
for beginning the war, and the settling of the plan of
operation.

Immediately after my arrival in Vienna, I went to
Count Stadion, who at that time was Minister for
Foreign Affairs.   He gave me an insight into the position : I found that war was nearer than I had supposed when I left Paris.   I explained to him my reasons for obtaining leave to come to Vienna, and gave
him to understand that it would be impossible for me
to be really useful to the important interests committed
to my care, if I were not thoroughly initiated into the
feeling of the Court.   Count Stadion showed the liveliest
satisfaction at coming to an understanding with me.
The next day I waited on the Emperor.   A conversation of many hours gave me the impression that the
Cabinet was more decided than the Emperor, not indeed
in respect to the war in itself, for with good reason it
was looked upon as unavoidable, but as to choosing
the right moment.   His Majesty charged me most
urgently to make myself acquainted with the steps
about to be taken, and to assist the cabinet with my
advice.

Emboldened by this request and the extraordinary
importance of the circumstances, I did not fail to explain
the situation exactly as it was.   My statement consisted of the following elements :—

The material preparations were nearly completed,

so that the army might, by the beginning of the year
1809, take the field. In this respect everything was
secured, and that to a degree which the enemy, if he
judged from the disasters of the campaign of 1805,
could not expect.

It was not so with the moral side of this great undertaking. I can testify that the cabinet was subject
to more than one illusion.

The change, made in the original plan of the campaign necessarily exercised an influence on the moral
side of the undertaking, which was quite as worthy of
being taken into account as the material operations,
when the state of men's minds in Germany was considered.* .   .   .   .

.   .   .   .

As I received no instructions from Vienna, I could
contribute little. Nothing could suit Napoleon better.
He continued, after my return, to treat me with his
customary kindness. The passive part I had to play
was a contrast to the excessive activity in the military
preparations, of which I was condemned to be a mere
spectator. If the Paris public judged from my relations to the Court, it must have been very difficult
for it to believe in the impending outbreak of a new
war with Austria. Napoleon liked to surprise the
Parisians, and to make known his wars only by the
cannons fired from the *Invalides* to announce the success
of the first battle. Willingly would I have hindered
him from acting so now; but this unhappily was not
permitted to me; for only by his unexpected departure
from Paris in the night of the 14th of April, and by
the message I received from Count Champagny on the
15th, that he had orders from his master to give me my

passports, did I learn that peace was at an end; the courier who ought to have brought me the news had been detained at Châlons-sur-Marne. By another courier the Minister for Foreign Affairs assured me, in the name of the Emperor, that the safety of my family would be cared for, in case I did not take them with me, but wished to leave them in Paris.

When I had fixed my departure for the 19th, the Postmaster-General de Lavalette * refused me horses, under the pretence that they were required for the Emperor's use. My repeated requests always met with the same refusal; and I was relieved from this state of uncertainty only by a letter from Count Champagny, which he sent to me from Munich on the 19th, in which he informed me that, the cause of the hindrances put in the way of my departure from Paris had been the arrest of the French agent and attaché in Vienna, and their being carried off to Hungary. At the same time he disclosed to me that till an exchange was made of the *personnel* of the embassy, I should not be allowed to leave Paris.

The measure, on the part of the Court of Vienna, was unusual, and also quite unnecessary; it originated in fear, and might have compromised my personal safety: the French ambassador had already come back from Vienna. This was, in my eyes, a fresh example of the false estimate the Austrian cabinet made of Napoleon's character and attitude. I remained quietly in Paris, and can certify from my own observations, how exceedingly weary France was of the war. The news

* One of the oldest adjutants of General Bonaparte. I had made his acquaintance at the Congress of Rastadt, at the beginning of which he was present. He it was whose wife, after the return of the Bourbons in 1815, aided him to escape out of prison when he was threatened with a fate like that of Marshal Ney and General Labédoyère.

of the very important events which attended the opening of the campaign were received in Paris with a
painful feeling, that already approached aversion to
the conqueror.   My life in society continued to be the
same as before the rupture : indeed, I might even maintain that the attentions of the public towards me rather
increased.

As I have reached that point of my narrative when
my office of Ambassador in France came to an end,
I think I may say a few words on the internal condition
of the country, and on some of the most prominent individuals of the time.

France felt the need of repose, and this feeling prevailed not only among the masses, but was shared by
Napoleon's companions in arms.   These individuals had
been for the most part taken from the lower ranks of the
army, and raised to the height of military honour.   They
had become rich from foreign spoil and the calculated
generosity of the Emperor, and now wished to enjoy
what they had gained.   Napoleon had made a brilliant existence for them.   The Prince of Neufchâtel
(Berthier) had a yearly income of more than 1,200,000
francs : Marshal Davoust had property which brought
in an income of a million : Masséna, Augereau, and
many other marshals and generals were equally wealthy.
These men wished to enjoy their possessions, and
objected to stake them on the chances of war.

Many in civil life had, like the generals, risen to
great wealth.   One source of riches, which during the
wars of the Revolution had existed for a class of specu-
lative spirits, was exhausted.   The war which Napoleon
declared against the fraudulent army-contractors, and
the strict order which he had introduced into all deal-
ings with the public money, reacted on this class,

already so numerous before Napoleon mounted the throne, and infused into them an aversion to the warlike policy, which formerly had the best wishes of themselves and those with whom they dealt. The nation, decimated by the annual levies, far from interesting itself in military operations carried on so far from the frontiers of France that even the names of the places where new victories were gained were unknown, cursed the conquests whose political value they were not capable of understanding. In a word, France was anxious for peace, and it was a great mistake of the European Courts at that time, that in their political action they did not take this fact into account. Napoleon was in power, but between the system followed by him and the feeling of the great country which he governed there was a repugnance of which the cabinets of Europe were not aware. It would have been wise if this had not been excluded from their calculations, which, in spite of all that the French manifestoes said on the subject, sprang only from the feeling of self-preservation in the European States. This remark explains my anxiety that, on the near approach of the war, the right course should be taken. The universal error in Europe arose from the fact that the vast encroachments made by the violent ambition of one man were supposed to spring from a national movement in France itself. I should hardly myself have seen this so clearly if I had not been placed in so favourable a position for observation.

The Emperor enjoyed, in France, that popularity which will be always gained by a ruler who knows how to hold the reins of power with an equally firm and skilful hand. Napoleon's practical mind enabled him to understand the needs of a country where the social

edifice had to be rebuilt. Abroad a soldier, at home he
was a legislator and most able administrator. Therefore the country lamented to see˙ him and his work
exposed to the chances of war. France was no longer
inspired by a warlike spirit. The revolutionary parties
alone, between 1792 and the beginning of the nineteenth century, entertained the idea of war. This they
did with the double object of employing beyond the
frontier the army, which was always a danger when at
home to this party, and of defending the frontiers against
foreign invasion. Had Napoleon confined his plans to
the preservation of what the Republic had conquered,
he would have greatly increased his popularity; his
warlike temperament carried him much further. He
was a born conqueror, legislator, and administrator, and
he thought he could indulge all three inclinations at
once. His undoubted genius furnished him with the
means of doing so. The sentiment of the enormous
majority of the nation would have been entirely with
him if he had confined himself to the duties of government.

The greater part of the high officials shared in this
national feeling. Among these were the Prince of Benevento (Talleyrand), Fouché, then Minister of Police, and
a great number of marshals and generals. The moral
power of the Emperor was too overpowering to be
opposed openly, therefore intrigue was resorted to, and
this was a means quite suited to the characters of the
two first-named personages. During the time that I
was ambassador, I had many opportunities of verifying
this fact.

Talleyrand possessed unusual intellectual ability.
My long-continued relations with him made me aware
that his whole character more adapted him to destroy

than to create. A priest, his temperament led him to irreligious courses. Of noble birth, he pleaded for the uprooting of his class; under the republican rule he foreswore the Republic; under the Empire he was constantly inclined to conspire against the Emperor; under the Bourbons, lastly, he laboured for the overthrow of the legitimate dynasty. To hinder any definite course from being taken—for that Talleyrand was always ready. In the contrary direction, I could never discover equal ability. Napoleon so estimated him, and with justice. In one of our conversations which took place in consequence of one of the many withdrawals of Talleyrand from the Ministry, the Emperor said to me: 'If I want anything done, I do not employ the Prince of Benevento; I turn to him when I want a thing not to be done which I wish to appear to want.' In private life, however, Talleyrand was as trustworthy as he was agreeable.

Fouché was a complete contrast to Talleyrand. In consequence of the contradictory character of the two men, the word 'rivalry' was not applicable to them. Their opposition was radical, for it had its source in difference of character. Fouché had been a priest, like Talleyrand, and had stained himself with blood and mire; while Talleyrand lost himself in the theories of that school which called itself the English School. Fouché was an enemy to all theories; he was a practical man, deterred by no obstacle. Thoroughly acquainted with the French mind, he went forward with the time, but always in extremes, convinced as he was that in this manner only an extreme end could be attained. Never had these two men any points of contact, unless their paths crossed in following out some conspiracy against the existing order of things. Napoleon knew both of them, and made use of their talents, as well as their faults, whenever he thought they could be useful to favour his own views. At the time of which I speak, Fouché, as Minister of Police, had gained the confidence of the *émigrés*, to whom Napoleon had re-opened the doors of France. He showed them all the services in his power, which seemed to bear the character of complete disinterestedness. Fouché foreboded the overthrow of the Emperor, and hence regarded the return of the Bourbons only as possible.

The man in whose talent for governing Napoleon had the most confidence was Cambacérès, and, therefore, when he took the field beyond the frontiers of France, he left the business affairs in his hands. More than once Napoleon analysed to me the peculiarities of the Arch-Chancellor, as they appeared to him. I had not the opportunity myself of forming an opinion with regard to Cambacérès, for he lived in seclusion, and never left it but on occasions of great ceremonial. At the beginning of the Revolution he sat as advocate in the Parliament of Aix in Provence, the President of which was M. d'Aigrefeuille. The advocate made his fortune, the president was ruined. The two being friends, Cambacérès took him into his house. When his protector was at the height of his power, D'Aigrefeuille filled the position of a servant. One day, when Cambacérès was invested with the dignity of *Archichancelier* of the kingdom—that fantastic imitation of the ceremonial of the old German Empire—to which the title ' Durchlaucht' (Serene Highness) was attached, D'Aigrefeuille addressed him for the first time with this title. ' When we are alone,' said Cambacérès to him, ' don't use these empty titles ; continue to treat me as a friend, and content yourself with calling me Monseigneur.'

When Napoleon made the first batch of Counts and
Barons, Cambacérès celebrated the event by a banquet,
to which he invited the ambassadors and first officials
of the kingdom. After dinner the newly ennobled came
to pay their respects to him. As the new titles were
announced, the reception-room was filled with laughter;
Cambacérès alone was imperturbable.

On May 16, Fouché wrote to me that, in consequence
of an order from the Emperor, he had to request me to
go to Vienna, to be there exchanged for some of the
personnel of the French embassy. He wished to know
the day I thought I could start, which he begged me to
hasten as much as possible, and added that an officer of
gendarmes would escort me on my journey. I named
the next day, but an inflammation in the eyes detained
me in Paris till the 26th. I took with me all the
officers of the embassy, and some Austrian travellers
who had been detained in Paris, who, but for this oppo-
tunity, might have found difficulty in leaving France.
I left my family in the hotel of the embassy. The progress made by the war and the siege of Vienna itself
led me to prefer this course to the chances of a difficult
journey. Besides, I knew the ground too well to be un-
easy as to the welfare of those I left behind me in Paris.

At Châlons-sur-Marne, I met the first train of Austrian prisoners, among whom were many officers of my
acquaintance. I hastened to hear the news from them,
but I had none to give them in exchange, for I had been
deprived of every source of information, except the
French army bulletins, since the beginning of the campaign. In Luneville a report was current that the
French had lost a decisive battle. In Strasburg I heard
this confirmed, it referred to the battle of Aspern. The
Empress Josephine was residing at the time in this city.

I had hardly alighted, when I received an invitation to go
to her in the course of the evening. I found her in great
anxiety as to the consequences the event might have.
She told me of circumstances, which she had learned,
which left me no doubt as to the importance of the
defeat. They seemed so decisive and exact that
Josephine did not doubt I should, on my arrival in
Vienna, find the negotiations for peace already begun.
The Empress went so far as to think I might meet
Napoleon returning to France! I mention this circumstance, because it shows how little confidence as to the
issue of this war was entertained in the very bosom
of the family of Napoleon.

On June 5 I arrived at Vienna, and went to the
Palais Esterhazy with Prince Paul, who was with me
as my attaché. I hastened to my father, whom I found
quite overwhelmed by an order he had just received,
to repair, with the Archbishop of Vienna and Counts
Pergen and Hardegg, to France, as hostages for the
payment of a contribution imposed on the city of
Vienna. My father was determined to yield to force
only, in which plan I encouraged him; while, on the
other hand, I took upon myself to dissuade Napoleon
from so false a measure. For this purpose I went, by
the permission of the Prince of Neufchâtel, direct to
the Emperor, and the so-called hostages remained in
the capital without further molestation. Napoleon laid
the blame on the Commissary-General.

The next morning I visited Champagny, in the
Burg, where the Empress had rooms, while the Emperor lived at Schönbrunn. The minister received me
with honied phrases, in which a great feeling of anxiety
was perceptible. In consequence of the battle of
Aspern, the position of the French army was quite

altered. Public spirit was roused once more in Vienna.
The precautions taken by the invading army were
redoubled. The time teemed with the most important
events, which were explained by the different parties
each in their own manner. There was no confidence
on the enemy's side. Champagny told me he had not
been informed on what day the officers of the French
embassy, who were to be sent in exchange, would be
at the place appointed, and begged me to wait in
patience for this moment. 'Think, meanwhile, on the
possible issue of the impending drama: you will find
the Emperor in good humour about it.' I answered,
that in my position, as prisoner, I had nothing to do
with business, and that I should await the arrangements
respecting my person very quietly. Champagny invited
me to dine with him on that day, and I found myself
in the enemy's camp, in the capacity of an unconcerned
spectator. Thus I had no opportunity to prepare myself for what was reserved for me in the time just at
hand.

On the morning of June 7, an adjutant of Count
Andrassy, then Governor of Vienna, came to me to
announce, in the name of the Emperor, that I could
not remain in Vienna; but that it was left to me to
await the moment of my exchange in any place I
preferred in the neighbourhood of the capital. I declared myself ready to obey the orders of the Emperor;
but I added, at the same time, that I was in reality not
a prisoner, and that the more painful he made my
position the more he would add to its injustice. I asked
to be allowed to go to a country house belonging to my
mother at Grünberg, a mile and a half from Vienna,
close to the garden of Schönbrunn. This choice was
accepted; and thither I repaired on the morning of the

8th. The officer of gendarmes, who came with me from
Paris, I took to live with me at Grünberg; and as I
would not have the officers of the embassy share my
uncomfortable position, I took only my necessary ser-
vants with me. During the whole time of my stay in
this house I was careful to behave as a prisoner; in
spite of the fine speeches of my jailers, I did not go
beyond the house.

Some days after my arrival in Grünberg, I heard
the sound of a horse in the front of my house. I ran
to the window and saw General Savary, who on seeing
me made as if he had not known that I was living
there, and jumping down from his horse, came in to
see me. Savary was chief of the police at head-
quarters,—an office which he filled, also, when the Emperor resided in Paris. Savary was at the head of one
division of police whose business it was to control that
which Fouché directed. The palaces inhabited by
Napoleon were under the guardianship of a third body
of police, at whose head was General Duroc.

General Savary did not hesitate to turn the conversation to politics, which he did apparently with candour, finding fault with the perpetual war, the dangers
of which for France itself he recounted, whilst he dwelt
on the necessity of obtaining a lasting foundation for
peace. I allowed him to deliver himself of all his phrases
without interrupting him; and when he saw my calmness and quietness, he said to me, ' Why do you not use
the opportunity of being in the Emperor's neighbourhood to obtain a meeting with him? You live two or
three steps from one another, the gardens are close
together : instead of taking the air in your own, go over
into the Schönbrunn garden; the Emperor will be de-
lighted to see you.'

'The pleasure,' I answered, 'would not be mutual; still that consideration would not keep me back. But I shall not go out of this place till the day when I receive the order to do so. I can do nothing by halves. If I am a prisoner, I behave myself as a prisoner; if I am free, I shall make use of my freedom; but if I had my freedom at this moment, I should certainly not use it in order to go and walk with Napoleon in the garden belonging to the Emperor my master.'

'You do not wish then to see the Emperor?' answered Savary. 'You would find him in the best and most peaceful disposition. A conversation between you might have the happiest consequences. You would perhaps obtain for the Emperor Francis some most important suggestions. I hope you do not confuse a certain proclamation with Napoleon's true feelings: those were words spoken to the winds.'

'I have nothing to say to your master, and nothing to hear from him,' said I to Savary. 'I am practically a prisoner, and prisoners of my kind consider themselves, if they do their duty, as dead.'

On my making this declaration, Savary left me. I did not doubt but that he had been commissioned by Napoleon to sound me with regard to a meeting; and if I had not had from the very beginning a presentiment that this was his purpose, a step made in this direction by the Minister of Foreign Affairs would have left me no doubt on the matter. On the second as well as the first occasion I refused the meeting, which would have been turned to account by Napoleon in a way which I had no right to allow to be done. It is evident that, looking at the position of the two armies, Napoleon wished to avoid the risks of a new battle, after that of Aspern, and would have been well pleased if he could have made use of me to induce the Imperial Cabinet to take the initiative in the interests of a peaceful settlement.

At the place in which I was interned I received visits from the most distinguished men of Vienna ; I thus learned the real position of the two armies, and could not doubt that we were standing on the eve of an event the result of which would be decisive of the fate of the campaign.   On the evening of June 17 Colonel Avy, a staff officer, came to me with a message from Marshal Berthier, that I was to go next morning to the place where the exchange was to be made, and that he was ordered to accompany me.   I therefore left Grünberg on the 18th.   In my escort I found the Attaché of the Parisian Embassy, Prince Paul Esterhazy and Count Mier, and the Counsellor of Legation Floret.   My *cortége* consisted of five carriages, which were escorted by fifty mounted Jägers.   We passed the night at the house of Count Harrach at Bruck, on the Leitha.   When we had arrived in Wieselburg on the 19th, Colonel Avy would not halt till he had received news of the arrival of the French *employé* at the outposts.   But when he learnt through an adjutant of the vice-King of Italy (Eugène Beauharnais) that the commandant of Komorn, General Davidovich, was quite uncertain on what day this agent would arrive, on account of the distance ; Avy declared that he had received orders to make the exchange on the 21st, and that if it were not accomplished, I must go back to Vienna, for he could not stay any longer at Wieselburg.   In fact, on the evening of the same day, I had to return to the house at Grünberg.   Napoleon immediately sent to apologise for what had taken place, by one of his adjutants, and to show me letters of the

Commandant of Komorn and Chief of the Staff to the vice-King, as a proof that there was neither mistake nor ill will on his part.

On June 26, Col. Avy came with the news that the French *employé* would be on the 28th at Acs, one of the places declared neutral, for twenty-four hours, for the purpose of making the exchange. We set off together at daybreak the following day, and arrived at Raab early on the 28th. On the way, I learned that Pressburg had been bombarded on the night of the 27th. After some hours' rest, we went, under an escort of fifty dragoons, to Acs, where I stopped with General Mont-brun, who commanded the outposts of the French army at this point. Opposite the place where, near to Gönyö, the high road runs along the banks of the Danube, an Austrian battery had been erected. The officer in command of it, when he saw a train of car-riages coming forward, guarded by a strong escort, thought it must be the retinue of the vice-King of Italy, and fired a volley at once. Although the zeal was mis-placed, I could not but do justice to the skill of our artillerymen. Of the first two shots, one went through the wheel of my carriage, the other passed two feet above the roof of it. Upon this, my escort left the high road, and took me as quickly as might be across the fields.

On the 29th, the *employé* not having arrived at the place of rendezvous, General Montbrun sent to Komorn to enquire after him. General Davidovich replied that M. Dodun would not be at the outposts for two or three days. On hearing this, Colonel Avy, on the 30th, took me back to Raab, by Bony, in order to avoid the famous battery at Gönyö. On the morning of July 1, Colonel Avy was informed by Prince Eugène, the chief

of the staff, that the French *employé* had reached Komorn, and would be at Acs by the afternoon at two
o'clock. We immediately went on our way again.
While going backwards and forwards in this way, I saw
a great movement take place in the French army. The
bodies of troops which I met were marching towards
Vienna. As no military event had taken place, I could
only suppose that Napoleon was preparing to strike a
blow.

On our arrival at Acs, at seven o'clock in the morning, we found the mansion empty which had been the
head-quarters of General Montbrun. The house-steward
whom I questioned, told me that the place had been
vacated the evening before, and was now occupied only
by a division of the Hungarian *'Aufstand.'* When Colonel
Avy received this news, he jumped out of my carriage,
and ran to the officer in command of the escort, ' Give
me the best horse you can spare ! ' I drew the Colonel
back ; ' You forget,' said I to him, ' that our parts are
exchanged. I have been under your protection ; now
you are under mine, national law protects you ; you
will not be made a prisoner.' At this moment an
Austrian officer of the staff appeared with an escort,
and informed us that the French *employé* was at the
place appointed for carrying out the exchange. I requested Colonel Avy to halt the escort, and to follow
me. We went to the place, where we found Dodun.
I joined the Austrian, he the French corps. I never
heard anything more of this diplomatist : Colonel Avy
was killed in Spain in 1810 or 1811. His personal
attention to me during the whole time of the perform-
ance of his thankless task should be mentioned with
praise.

In Komorn I met the Archduke Palatin, who took

the command of the Hungarian '*Aufstand.*' I learned
from him that the Emperor Francis was waiting at
Wolkersdorf with impatience till I could join him. I
spent the night in Komorn, and reached Wolkersdorf
on the evening of July 3.

The Emperor received me with the hearty kindness
which he had already showed me so abundantly. He
told me all that had happened since my departure from
Vienna in the last days of the previous year. Quiet
and firm as ever, he was yet penetrated with the difficulty of the situation, daily expecting an event decisive
of the war. The movement which I had observed in
the enemy's army corresponded with this expectation.
His majesty informed me that he intended to keep me
with him during the rest of the campaign.

After I left the Emperor, I hastened to Count Stadion,
and found him quite overwhelmed and ready to give
up the situation as lost. Count Stadion was one of
those men of lively imagination and quick understanding,
who are easily overcome by the impressions of the moment. Men of this sort always incline to extremes;
for them there are no transitions, and since these nevertheless do exist, when they come before them instead
of knowing how to wait, they too often act at random.
The minister acknowledged that the policy which I pro-
pounded would have accomplished more, if it had been
followed. Although I agreed with him on this point,
I assured him that I ascribed the misfortunes which had
fallen on our empire, and the extreme danger in which
it was placed, not merely to any specified plan of operations: the true causes were rather the unhappy choice
of the moment for the rising, and the inaction of the
army after the victory of May 22. Count Stadion told
me that he only waited the result of a battle on the left

bank of the Danube to decide the question whether
he should continue to serve or not—a battle which the
Archduke Charles was expecting, and which in fact appeared to be immediately impending, to judge from the
preparations made by the French army to effect the
passage of the Danube.

July 4 passed in preparations for a battle. I was
with the Emperor when an envoy from the Archduke
came to inform him of the operations of the enemy,
and that his Imperial Highness was determined to await
the event with resolution. ' Tell my brother,' answered
the Emperor to the adjutant, ' that I am of opinion
that the enemy should not be allowed to cross in
force, and that it, would be well to drive those who
had crossed into the river.' This day there were only
partial fights between the advanced troops. In the following night, under a sharp cannonade, the French
army left the island, and went along the Lobau and
crossed that arm of the Danube, farther down the river
at Orth and two other points.

On the morning of July 5, I joined the Emperor on
the battle-field, on which the fate of the Empire was to
be decided. The battle was soon general, and we did
not return to Wolkersdorf till nightfall, amid the blazing
buildings which covered the Marchfeld. When we repaired to our post of observation in the grey of the early
morning of the next day, we witnessed the apparently
decisive result of the right wing of our army. About
one o'clock in the afternoon, however, Count Colleredo,
a general-adjutant of the Archduke's, came with the information to the Emperor, that his Imperial Highness
had ordered the retreat of the army. Without losing
his self-possession, the Emperor asked the messenger,
whether the Archduke had only determined on the

retreat, or whether it had actually commenced. When
the Emperor heard that the army was already in full
retreat, he said to the adjutant, 'Very well;' and
added, turning to me, 'We shall have much to retrieve.'
His Majesty gave immediate orders to remove his head-
quarters to Znaim. We remained some time on the
heights which commanded the broad plain of the Marchfeld, in front of Wolkersdorf, and then began our march,
which brought us to Ernstbrunn, where we passed the
night. On the following day we continued our retreat
to Znaim.

Count Stadion, Austrian diplomat and statesman. Metternich
replaced Stadion at the Foreign Ministry in 1809.

The Austrian chancellery building in Vienna.

CHAPTER V.

METTERNICH BECOMES MINISTER OF FOREIGN AFFAIRS.

(1809.)

ON the morning of July 8, 1809, I was sent for by the Emperor. He received me with the following words: 'Count Stadion has just given in his resignation; I commit the department of Foreign Affairs to you in his place.'

I begged his Majesty not to consider this appointment as definite. 'Two reasons,' said I, 'move me to make this request: one is, that this is not a favourable moment for changing the ministry; the other, to my mind no less important, that I do not consider myself

.fit for this post.   Neither my inclination nor my
talents, so far as I know them, qualify me for the high
functions which your Majesty wishes to confide to me.
This feeling is not based on the difficulties of the
moment, but on the knowledge which I have of myself.
I do not think myself capable of steering the vessel of
the state in so great an Empire; I do not wish to do
as I have seen done by far more able men than I am.
I should run the risk of advising badly, and my conscience does not allow me to bring this danger upon
your Majesty and the state.   Besides, the retirement of
Count Stadion from the ministry on the second day
after the battle of Wagram would have an importance
as seeming to imply an abandonment by your Majesty
of the cause for which you have already made so many
sacrifices; I should regard this step as a great mistake.'
      With the patience which never left him in the
greatest crises—and what monarch has gone through
more than the Emperor Francis?—with a strength of
mind and firmness of character which comprise all the
gifts most valuable for princes who are called to govern,
the Emperor answered : 'What you say of Stadion's
resignation under present circumstances is quite true;
but he has insisted, and I have accepted his resignation,
because you cannot urge a man to remain in a position which he wishes to leave, when it calls upon him
to administer important business.   As to the difficulties
which you raise about taking the office yourself, the
same rule does not apply to you; far from being deterred
by the considerations you mention, I am confirmed
by them in my choice.   I am less afraid of men who
doubt their own capacity than of those who think
themselves fit for everything.   I count on the know-
'ledge you have of the difficulties of the position, and on

your patriotism. . Confer, then, with Count Stadion on the most suitable method of making the change of ministry ; and come back and inform me when you have agreed what to do.'

'I will do what your Majesty commands,' I replied ; 'still, I beg your Majesty to believe that my disinclination has nothing to do with the present crisis, but rests on quite other grounds ; and in case Count Stadion will not on my representation remain in office, may I beg your Majesty to grant me a favour, namely, that your Majesty will promise to dismiss me on the day when your Majesty sees me going wrong ? '

'That I promise you,' answered the Emperor, 'but I hope that this contingency will not occur to either of us.'

I went immediately to Count Stadion, whom I found immovable in his resolution to retire. Great determination was one of the characteristic features of this minister : and if this quality had not been marred by a most dangerous precipitation, the war of 1809 would not have taken place under such auspices as it did. As I saw that my efforts to make him change his resolution were fruitless, I turned our conversation in a direction in which Count Stadion's high feeling did not allow me to fear a defeat. I appealed to his feeling of duty, and pointed out the consequences which his sudden resignation must have. The result was that we agreed to propose to the Emperor that he should order the Archduke Charles to continue the retreat of the army under his command towards Bohemia, and that Count Stadion should remain as minister with the Archduke. His Majesty should put himself at the head of the army in Hungary ; and I should accompany the Emperor, performing *ad interim* the functions of a Minister of Foreign

Affairs in attendance on his person. Lastly, we agreed that the actual retirement of Count Stadion from the ministry should be delayed till the end of the war, on the issue of which it should depend. We went both together to the Emperor, who was satisfied with the arrangement.

I here avow with all sincerity that there was nothing in me to counterbalance the load of responsibility which was laid upon me but the feeling of duty. Free from the stimulus of ambition, as I have been all my life, I felt only the weight of the fetters which were to rob me of my personal freedom, and was, with more sensitiveness than was natural to me, weighed down under the influence of my new position.

Soon after this conclusion had been arrived at, the Emperor left Znaim, and I accompanied him to Hungary. We took the road over the Jablunka Pass, and went straight to Komorn. Count Stadion attached himself to the Archduke Charles. I travelled from Znaim to Komorn in the Emperor's carriage, and I made use of the time to lay before his Majesty my view of the present position of affairs. From this prince's calm and just line of thought, from the impression made on me by his strong and candid mind, I was convinced that in all important questions my views would always be in harmony with his, and that his great qualities would ever insure me the support without which a minister, be his views ever so good, can make no certain plan and carry out no project with prospect of success. We examined the situation of the empire with thorough impartiality; we reviewed the prospects which the war still presented, as well as those promised by a peace concluded under the most unhappy auspices.

Shortly after the arrival of the Emperor at Komorn

we received the details of the battle of Znaim, and the news of a truce between the two armies. At the same time there came to me a proposal from Count Champagny, for the opening of negotiations for peace.

I found the Emperor inclined to the reception of this offer, and I therefore settled with the French Minister that our meeting should take place at the town of Altenburg, in the province of Wieselburg. On this occasion there arose a singular difficulty in a matter of form. I did not know what title to take in order to address my answer to Count Champagny in the third person. My name alone would be of no authority. I was no longer an ambassador, and not yet a minister. I informed the Emperor of the difficulty, and he ruled that I should take the title of Minister of State.

As the town of Altenburg was chosen for the negotiations, and as it lay within the French line of demarcation according to the Treaty of Znaim, it was declared neutral. The Emperor took up his abode at Totis, where soon afterwards Prince John Liechtenstein, commander-in-chief of the army, had his head-quarters. This prince had taken the command from Archduke Charles, who had gone back to Teschen. General Count Bubna held the office of military commissary with Napoleon. Since I was entrusted with the functions of Chief Plenipotentiary for the peace negotiations, I begged the Emperor to appoint an influential military officer as second Plenipotentiary. The choice fell on General Count Nugent, who during the campaign had acted as quartermaster-general to the corps commanded by the Archduke John.

The knowledge which I had gained of the men with whom I was to negotiate such important interests did not allow me to consider the negotiation as a serious matter on Napoleon's part. He wanted to get his army into condition again, after the successes bought by such great sacrifices. He knew that the Austrian forces also needed to be recruited; if he had not felt that a halt was needed in the operations, he would have followed up his advantage. I did not expect therefore anything more from the Altenburg Conference than that it would either lead to the renewal of hostilities or be concluded by a peace dictated by Napoleon in his usual manner. The instructions which I took with me to the place of meeting were of a simple nature. My task was limited to exposing the moral position, that the Emperor should be forced to a definite conclusion, whether it were in favour of concluding the war or of carrying it on.

Since I do not intend to enter here into the details of this pretended negotiation, during which both armies were drawn up opposite each other, and only engaged in reinforcing themselves as much as possible, I will confine myself to mentioning one fact which characterised the political action of Napoleon and the servility of his agents.

I opened the negotiations with the request that they might be divided into formal sittings, conducted by Protocols and into simple conversations without anything of the kind. Count Champagny said he was not authorised to use protocols, still he was ready to inform his master of my request. Although the distance was so short which separated the place from Napoleon's headquarters at Schönbrunn, days passed by without any answer from him. When at last it came, it was in the negative. I now explained that I did not call the conversations between Plenipotentiaries a negotiation, and that they could only prepare the way for such. In this

way the discussions went on for about fourteen days, when
suddenly, in consequence of the arrival of a courier from
Schönbrunn, Count Champagny sent me a note, in which
he informed me that the Emperor, his master, having
taken into consideration the advantages which would be
gained by adopting the proposed form, not only agreed
to the drawing up of Protocols, but also wished that the
Protocols already prepared might be laid before me for
approval, in order that the conferences with a view to
peace already held might not be lost time. There were,
in fact, a number of reports of conferences which were
never held enclosed with the note of the French Plenipotentiary. I answered Count Champagny, that I was not
accustomed to make use of any other pen than my own
in the expression of my thoughts on so grave an occasion, and should not condescend to put my signature
to worthless documents ; but I was ready to consider
the so-called Protocols as containing what had been said
by the French Plenipotentiaries ; although with the em-
phatic proviso, that my words therein should be replaced
by authentic documents, which I was ready to supply.
On this declaration Count Champagny withdrew his proposal. The false Protocols contained only reports which
were written in a spirit which Napoleon permitted in order
that, in the event of hostilities being renewed, their character might be changed into that of manifestoes. I
asked Count Champagny how he could take upon himself
to make me such a proposal, which the plainest common
sense must know to be a futile and compromising attempt. He excused himself with the assurance that
it was not he who had thought of it ; the pretended
Protocols were dictated by Napoleon himself, and he
must admit that he neither had said to me anything of
the matter of the acts in question nor had heard any-

thing like it from my mouth. 'Napoleon,' I remarked to him, ' has the power of putting words into your mouth which your position prevents you perhaps from deny-ing ; but what he can do with you, he cannot do to me —he may conquer kingdoms, but never my conscience!'

Several days more passed in the inaction described, and my anticipations with regard to Napoleon's proceed-ings were verified.

Count Bubna, who, as already mentioned, was Mili-tary Commissary at Napoleon's head-quarters, was or-dered by him to request the Emperor Francis to send Prince John Liechtenstein to Vienna. ' The diplo-matists,' added Napoleon, ' do not know how to get through an affair like the present; we soldiers under-stand one another better. Let the Emperor send Prince Liechstentein to me, and we will end the matter in four-and-twenty hours. I will tell him what I wish and what I desire from the Emperor ; and what I want he will grant me, because he is upright and wise. I desire—not the destruction of Austria—but its con-solidation. What I said against the Emperor Francis at the beginning of the war was nothing but a phrase ; such things are allowable before a battle, they vanish with the smoke of the cannon.'

I was informed of the sending for Field-Marshal Prince Liechtenstein, through an adjutant who pre-ceded him, with the request to make known his arrival at Vienna. The Prince was close behind him, and stopped to see me at Altenburg. He brought me a letter from the Emperor Francis, telling me that this mission had no other object but to arrive at last at a knowledge of Napoleon's intentions ; the Field-Marshal had orders to listen to everything, but not to enter into a discussion on any subject. When the Prince had informed me of the instructions he had received, I said to him, 'If I had been aware of your mission, rather than you should have passed the outposts of the French army I would have taken upon myself to request you to wait, till I had spoken to the Emperor. We are·no longer in Altenburg; you are within reach of the hostile army, and must go on. But I tell you beforehand that of two things one will happen: either Napoleon will lead you to do something that will compromise our cause; or he will prevent you from returning to your post. The army must have its commanders; this Napoleon knows, and has drawn you away from it. He will either constrain the Emperor to conclude a peace which he ought not to conclude, or he will deprive him of the means of carrying on the war.' The Prince, who was much agitated by what I said, declared he was ready to go back to Totis. I showed him that he must perform the commission he had undertaken, but must make every effort not to depart from it.

I feel bound in conscience to give here some account of Prince John Liechtenstein, one of the noblest characters of this sad time. He was a born soldier; he had not the qualities which make a statesman. With overflowing zeal for what is right, gifted with unusual faculties of mind, and a courage proof against every trial; a warm patriot, ready for any sacrifice, but without that balance which is necessary to learn the true value of men and things: he had already, in the year 1805, succumbed to the power which Napoleon was able to exercise in so high a degree upon those whom his interest required him to influence. Prince John saw in Napoleon only the mere soldier; in this quality he thought he was his equal. He deceived himself, and could not escape from the craft of a man who

united in himself the most different qualities in the
most extraordinary manner.

When the Field-Marshal had returned to Altenburg,
I went to Count Champagny and informed him that
as several days must pass without anything being done,
I thought of going back to Totis, but that I was
ready to return to Altenburg whenever the first news
in consequence of the arrival of Prince Liechtenstein
was received from Vienna at the French head-quarters.
'This news,' I continued, 'will, however, announce the
breaking off of the Altenburg negotiations.'   Count
Champagny would not admit my pre-supposition.   I
hastened the next morning to the Emperor, and went to
Totis to Count Stadion, who had arrived there from
Bohemia a short time before.

I did not conceal my fears from the Emperor; and
was convinced that in sending for Prince Liechtenstein,
the Emperor had yielded only from confidence in the
engagements entered into by Napoleon, and in consequence of a cabinet council which had decided in
favour of the attempt.   Before his departure from Totis,
Prince Liechtenstein had, in the fulfilment of the duties
required of him, made all preparations for the re-
sumption of hostilities.   Therefore I had only to maintain an observant and passive attitude; Count Stadion
had consented also, in case of a rupture, again to lead
the Ministry.

On the day after my return to the Emperor, I received the notice from Count Champagny that Napoleon
had just summoned him to Vienna; in consequence of
which, the Altenburg negotiation must be considered as
broken off.

Several days passed without any news from Vienna.
Prince Liechtenstein informed the Emperor of his plea-

sant reception by Napoleon, with the addition that,
nevertheless, Napoleon had refused to go into the subject of his summons, and referred him rather to the
Duke of Bassano (Maret), head of the personal cabinet
of the Emperor.

I concluded from this that my other foreboding
would shortly be fulfilled. From this time I directed
all my attention to the preparations for war. The
means we had at command were immense. The demon-
strations of the Russian army on the Galician side gave
me no uneasiness. I encouraged the Emperor only to
look forward. The patience of the Emperor was exhausted; his Majesty resolved on the recal of Prince
Liechtenstein, and I was commissioned to make the
necessary arrangements and preparations.

On October 14, towards evening, as I was walking
along the road from Totis towards Vienna, I saw car-
riages approaching, which I knew to be those of Prince
John Liechtenstein. As soon as the Prince saw me,
he stopped the carriage, jumped out, and said, 'I bring
you peace, and my head too: the Emperor will dispose
at his pleasure of both one and the other.'

This is what had happened in Vienna. Napoleon,
as before mentioned, had declined to speak to Prince
Liechtenstein himself on the matter for which he came,
and had referred him to the Duke of Bassano. The
Duke, for his part, declared to the Field-Marshal that
he was not Minister of Foreign Affairs, and that he must
wait the arrival of Count Champagny, whom the
Emperor had appointed to carry on the negotiation.
Prince Liechtenstein persisted in his protestation that he
was not commissioned with any negotiation. The Duke
of Bassano paid no regard to what he said. 'You will
talk over the affair with Champagny,' said he, 'and

easily come to an understanding with a man so pacific in his nature and so thoroughly acquainted with the Emperor's mind.' On the remark of the Field-Marshal that the place for peace negotiations was Altenburg, the Duke of Bassano replied that the Emperor, his master, had recalled his Plenipotentiary from that place, because it was not possible to carry on negotiations in two places! Prince Liechtenstein on that declared he should leave Vienna at once. 'You cannot do that,' replied the duke: 'the Emperor would regard it as a sign of breaking the truce; by doing so, you would compromise the fate of the army, and also of your country: and what is needed to avert from you so fearful a responsibility? A short delay, to learn what Napoleon thinks of proposing to the Emperor your master!' Finding himself in this dilemma, Prince Liechtenstein decided on remaining.

After the arrival of Count Champagny, the conferences began, under the name of Preliminaries, which were concluded on the night of October 13 and 14 with the signing of a document which the French Minister called the 'Project for a Treaty of Peace,' to be brought before the Emperor of Austria. After signing this document, which Prince Liechtenstein thought had this and no other meaning, he returned home at 5 o'clock in the morning; he had ordered his post-horses for 10 o'clock, when he suddenly at daybreak heard the firing of cannons, and on asking what this firing meant, was told it announced the signing of peace in the capital of Austria. He wished to make Napoleon answer for this on the spot, but Napoleon had just left Schönbrunn with all his retinue!

This is the history of the Peace of Vienna of October 14, 1809, and is known to only a limited circle: a

Treaty of Peace full of unworthy artifices, having no foundation in international rights.

The Emperor's decision under the circumstances could not be doubted. Without compromising himself and his Empire in the most dangerous manner, he could not reject the conclusion of a peace which had been already announced, amid the rejoicings of the people, in the capital and in more than a third part of the country still remaining to him. The Emperor ratified the treaty.

By this event the provisional character of the functions assigned to me at once terminated. I appeared now in the character of a Minister of Foreign Affairs ; and frankly admit that I took possession of the portfolio with more self-confidence than I had expected in the previous July. What had just taken place disclosed a side of Napoleon to me which placed him far lower in my eyes; and before my conscience the cause I had to uphold rose in like measure.

At the end of November, I came with the Emperor back to Vienna, and alighted at the Chancellor's Palace.

The conditions of the act of October 14 were loyally carried out in all directions. The places of the Empire occupied by the French forces and those of the Confédération of the Rhine were vacated, and the war contribution discharged within the appointed time. The return of the Emperor to his capital was like a triumphal entry. The populace there, as in the provinces, did not look beyond the present moment, satisfied with being relieved from the presence of an enemy who carried refinement, in making use of all the resources of the country, to the very highest degree. Napoleon, in the eyes of Europe, passed for an irresistible power, under the yoke of which all must bow. The feeling of the masses was no longer to escape this fate, but to lighten the burden as much as possible. My thoughts, however, soared higher. Under the load of enormous responsibility, I found only two points on which it seemed possible to rest, the immovable strength of character of the Emperor Francis, and my own conscience.

The results of the rising of Austria in the year 1809 were most destructive for the Empire. The (so-called) Peace of Vienna had bound the kingdom with a circle of iron, deprived it of its communication with the Adriatic, and from Brody, the north-east point of junction with Russia, to its south-east boundary adjoining the Ottoman Empire, encircled it with countries which were under the sceptre of Napoleon, or subject to his direct influence. The Empire accordingly lost all freedom of movement; and the conqueror had done all that lay in his power to hinder any future development of strength, by a secret article in the Treaty of Peace, which limited the maximum of the Austrian forces to a hundred and fifty thousand men.

Called to the hard task of defending the political existence of the Empire under such adverse circumstances, I compared the position of the European continent and the peculiar situation of the Austrian States, and, weighing the evils which pressed upon each, carefully watched for the preponderating influence.

I considered the Revolution, as it burst forth in France in 1789, as the starting-point of all the misfortunes of Europe, and I clearly perceived that a military despotism, which found its highest expression in Napoleon, was its inevitable result. If the wars occasioned by the Revolution had preserved Germany and Austria from the infection of social theories, during the twenty years which had elapsed between 1789 and 1809—

for nations are averse to adopt as benefits those doctrines which are presented to them by the force of
arms—I at the same time recognised in Napoleon himself a barrier against the encroachments of anarchical
theories in France and in those countries upon which lay
the weight of his iron arm.   Social questions, therefore,
I placed in the background, but in the very first rank
I placed the preservation of what remained of the
Austrian Empire, even after its unsuccessful campaigns.
That Napoleon, in his lust of power on the European
continent, had already overstepped the limits of the
possible—of this I had not the slightest doubt.   I fore-
saw that neither he nor his undertakings would escape
the consequences of rashness and extravagance.   The
when and the *how* I could not pretend to determine.
Thus my reason pointed out to me the direction which
I had to take in order not to interfere with the natural
development of the situation, and to keep open for
Austria the chances which the greatest of all powers,
the power of circumstances, might offer sooner or later
(under the strong government of its monarch) for the
much-threatened prosperity of the Empire.   As it was
beyond everything necessary to await the development
of events after the return of Napoleon to his capital, I
made use of the leisure so gained to go to Vienna and
make myself acquainted with the requirements of the
departments which had been entrusted to me.   I gave
the Chancellery an inner organisation more fitted to the
times ; in doing which I had before my mind the former
organisation under Prince Kaunitz.

In accordance with my proposal, the Emperor Francis
had appointed Prince Schwarzenberg, Ambassador in
France : a better choice could not have been made, as
events proved.

Neither before nor after the conclusion of the Vienna Peace had a single word been exchanged between Napoleon and the Austrian Cabinet regarding the design of the Emperor of the French as to his marriage. We were aware of the negotiations with the Russian Court, which Napoleon had entered into for a marriage with one of the Grand-Duchesses, and we also knew that Napoleon had decided to dissolve his marriage with the Empress Josephine, that marriage being without canonical authority. But we were so little aware of his intentions with regard to an Austrian Archduchess, that when the first indications of it came to us from the expressions of Mr de Laborde, we regarded it as a fantastic dream, and on. attributed a serious character to the matter when Napoleon himself, on the occasion of a ball, asked my wife, who had remained behind in Paris, to make known his intentions to me.

At a masked ball, at Cambacérès', to which my wife had received a very pressing invitation, a mask, in whom she immediately recognised Napoleon, took hold of her arm, and led her into a private room at the end of the suite of apartments. After some jokes of no importance, Napoleon asked her, whether she thought that the Archduchess Marie Louise would accept his hand, and whether the Emperor, her father, would agree to this alliance. My wife, very much surprised by this question, assured him that it was impossible for her to answer it. On that, Napoleon asked further whether she, in the place of the Archduchess, would bestow her hand upon him. My wife assured him she would refuse him. 'You are cruel!' said the Emperor to her; 'write to your husband, and ask him what he thinks of the matter.' My wife refused to do this, and pointed out that Prince Schwarzenberg was the organ through which he should approach the Imperial Court. Neither did she delay to inform the Ambassador, who was present at the ball, of what had passed between her and the Emperor.

The following morning, Prince Eugène made his appearance at Prince Schwarzenberg's, and in ' the name of the Emperor and with the knowledge of his mother, the Empress Josephine,' he made the same offer, which, the Ambassador explained, he could only receive *ad referendum.*

As soon as the courier brought me this news, I repaired to the Emperor. ' Your Majesty,' said I, ' is here placed in a situation in which the Ruler and the Father can alone say Yes or No. One or the other must be spoken by you, for a doubtful or hesitating answer is not possible.'

The Emperor collected himself for a moment, and then asked me what I should do in his place.

' There are cases in the life of states as with private persons,' I answered, ' when a third person is not able to put himself in the place of another, on whom the responsibility of a decision rests. These cases are especially those in which calculation alone is not sufficient to lead to a decision. Your Majesty is Ruler and Father—to you alone it belongs to consider what is your duty.'

' I shall leave the decision in my daughter's hands,' cried the Emperor, warmly ; ' for I will never constrain her, and I desire, before I consult my duty as a monarch, to know what is her wish in the matter. Find the Archduchess, and let me know what she says to you. I will not myself speak to her on the subject, lest it should seem as if I wished to influence her decision.'

I went at once to the Archduchess Marie Louise, and laid the matter before her, without circumlocution or fine phrases, either for or against the proposal. The Archduchess listened with her usual calmness, and after a moment's reflection, asked me, ' What does my father wish ? '

' The Emperor,' I replied, ' has commissioned me to interrogate your Imperial Highness as to your decision in a matter so important for the destiny of your whole life. Do not ask what the Emperor wishes : tell me what you wish.'

' I wish only what it is my duty to wish,' answered the Archduchess ; ' where the interest of the Empire is concerned that interest must be consulted, and not my will. Ask my father to consult his duty as a ruler, and to subordinate to that any interests connected with my person.'

When I reported this result of my mission to the Emperor, he said to me, with that perfect openness which was usual to him in the most difficult circumstances, ' I am not surprised at what you tell me from my daughter ; I know she is too good for me to expect her to do otherwise. Whilst you have been with her I have been thinking how to decide. My consent to the marriage would secure to the Empire some years of political peace, which I can devote to the healing of its wounds. All my powers are devoted to the welfare of my people, I cannot, therefore, hesitate in my decision. Send a courier to Paris, and say, that I accept the offer for the hand of my daughter, but with the express reservation, that on neither side shall any condition be attached to it ; there are sacrifices which must not be contaminated with anything approaching to a bargain.'

This is the truth with regard to the marriage of Napoleon with the Archduchess Marie Louise.

When Napoleon sounded Prince Schwarzenberg whether any concessions on his side would be agreeable to the Emperor, the Ambassador was in a position to express himself in the same sense as the Emperor himself had done.

One question which naturally had a great interest for the public was the divorce of Napoleon and Josephine. For the Church this question did not exist, and therefore not for the Emperor. Napoleon had contracted a civil marriage with the express understanding that the union could be dissolved ; in the eyes of the Church, therefore, it was not a valid marriage. Indeed, had it been otherwise, the scheme could not have been entertained for a moment. The dissolution of the first marriage, so called, had only, therefore, the value of a mere formality such as the French civil law required.

That this event, however, drew a line between the past and the present is quite evident. I felt myself called to direct my gravest attention to the future ; and I think that I fulfilled this duty to the best of my power.

Talleyrand, the accomplished French diplomat.

The Empress Marie Louise, Napoleon's second wife.

Prince Schwarzenberg, Austrian general and, in 1810, Ambassador
at Paris.

CHAPTER VI.

SPECIAL MISSION TO PARIS.

(1810.)

THE step which Napoleon had taken must have had a motive, and I now considered it my next and most important task to discover and follow up the Emperor's reasons. Napoleon's union with the Austrian Imperial family was doubtless the result of some calculation. What could be its aim?

Will the Imperial conqueror put his sword in its sheath and build up the future of France, and of his family, on the principles of internal order and external peace?

Or does the soldier-Prince desire, with the help of Austria, to found a dynasty, and at the same time continue his system of conquest?

The answers to these questions would decide our action in the future. The first of these queries did

not seem to me, from the character of Napoleon, to be
probable, the other rested on such impracticable sup-
positions that I could not build on it with any certainty,
however well it· corresponded with the habits of that
prince.   I therefore decided to request the Emperor to
allow me to go to Paris at the same time as the new
Empress, and to remain there till I could discover the
true state of the case.   The Emperor agreed to my
proposal, and forthwith I prepared to carry it out.

Marshal Berthier, on whom the title of Prince of
Neufchâtel and Wagram had been conferred, was sent
to Vienna with the proposal for the hand of the Archduchess Marie Louise.   Archduke Charles, entrusted with
Napoleon's Procuration, represented the bridegroom at
the altar, and the formal giving up of the Empress took
place at Braunau, where she was received by the Queen
of Naples, Napoleon's sister.   The Austrian people took
the event with that feeling which, after long wars and
boundless sacrifices, greets every prospect of peace as a
blessing ; they looked upon it as a pledge of peace.
Neither the Emperor nor I went so far in our hopes ;
mine were limited to the obtaining of an interval of
quiet for the recruiting of our resources for the possibility of a necessary defence of the interests of the
Empire.

In order not to take the same road as the Empress
Marie Louise, who went by the south of Germany and
Strasburg to Paris, I chose the road by Metz to Compiègne, whither I had been invited by Napoleon.   At
that place I was joined by Prince Schwarzenberg and
my wife, who had arrived there from Paris.   The members of the Imperial family were all assembled in the
palace which the Emperor had had prepared with the
greatest magnificence to receive his new consort.   At

the moment when I arrived, Napoleon had just left it
to meet the Empress : I was not, therefore, received by
him till after their first meeting.

Napoleon welcomed me with visible signs of satisfaction. He expressed his gratification at the conclusion
of the event which at this moment occupied him entirely; he touched on all the details of the course of
the negotiation, and came back to the point, that we
must omit nothing which could make the happy event
of the moment as sweet and pleasant as possible. He
spoke to me of an entire forgetfulness of the past, of
a happy and peaceful epoch, at which we had now
arrived, of the impossibility that anything should dis-
turb the natural relations between us ; on which I expressed the wish that during my residence in Paris I
might venture to speak on many subjects of great
importance for us, and of common utility for the two
empires.

The ecclesiastical details with respect to the affair
of the divorce brought the conversation to the existing
dispute with the Holy See, and I felt myself called upon
not to refuse our good offices between Pope Pius VII.
and Napoleon. That this step, in the main, led to no
result does not prevent me from mentioning it here.

Napoleon spoke too of the last war, and during this
conversation many interesting admissions fell from him.
'If,' so he said among other things, 'in the month of
September you had recommenced hostilities and beaten
me, I should have been *lost*;' and when he saw that
he had said too much, he withdrew the word '*lost*'
and replaced it by 'in great difficulties.' But I would
not let it pass, but assured him I held by his first
expression, and this conviction had much strengthened
me in my attitude at Altenburg. I thanked him per-

sonally for having excused me at the time of the negotiations at Vienna, and assured him that I should never have concluded the last peace. 'Well, what would you have done then?' interrupted Napoleon.

'I would have made a far better peace, and one more in correspondence with our true strength; if not, then war.'

' War!' said the Emperor, taking up the word; 'then you would have done wrong: it would have been difficult to drive me out of Vienna; but a better peace than your negotiators at Schönbrunn succeeded in obtaining—that I believe.'

Accounts had just arrived which announced that Napoleon's marriage was very ill received at St. Petersburg. I was not at all surprised at this, though somewhat disturbed; for what we wished, I remarked, was simply peace and quiet, and it did not fall within our plans that Russia should be involved.

' What do you mean by that?' asked Napoleon.

' Russia is afraid,' I answered, 'and acts under the influence of fear : she is afraid of France, she fears our relations with France, and will quarrel out of sheer uneasiness and anxiety.'

' Do not be anxious,' interrupted Napoleon, ' if the Russians try to commit themselves. I will act as if I did not understand them.' With that he expatiated at length on his relations with that Power, from which I saw that much wisdom and care on the side of Austria would be necessary to prevent a rupture with Russia.

After a short stay in the Imperial Palace at Compiègne, I betook myself to Paris, where the Emperor had placed the Hôtel of Marshal Ney, with a complete household, at my disposal, which, however, I only used on very particular occasions.   I did not wish to burden the court with my family, so I generally resided in the house in the Chaussée d'Antin, which my wife had occupied since my departure from Paris in 1809.

The Empress Marie Louise was received by the French public with the same feeling which the marriage had called forth in Austria.   France was tired of war. After so many disastrous battles, conquerors and conquered joined in longing and hoping for a final settlement.   I saw proofs of this in all classes of the people, and more particularly in Napoleon's own family.

In the subsequent conversations which I had with the Emperor, he was warm in his declarations of goodwill to Austria.   As a special sign of his favour, Napoleon proposed to Prince Schwarzenberg (then Austrian Ambassador in Paris) and me to abolish the mediatisation of our families, and to enrol them as sovereign members of the Rhenish Confederation, a proposal which we both, in consideration of our official position, declined in the most polite manner.

In my intercourse with the Emperor, we took up again the thread of the conversation, so to speak, where it had been broken off before the war.   I had not come, however, to study the past, but to get a glimpse of the future; and since I wished to do this as quickly as possible, I one day remarked to the Emperor that my stay in Paris could not be of much longer duration. 'Your Majesty,' said I to him, ' sent me as a prisoner to Austria : I come back to Paris a free man, but yet not free from difficult duties.   Loaded as I am with an enormous responsibility, I have my duties in Vienna to fulfil.   The Emperor Francis wished me to accompany his daughter into France ; I have come by his orders, but it must be evident to you that my wish goes beyond this, and I would gladly find a guiding principle for my political action in a more remote future.'

'I understand you,' answered Napoleon : 'your wish corresponds with my own. Stay with us a few weeks, and you will leave us with satisfaction.'

These words might have led me to hope that my residence in Paris would not be much prolonged, but I knew Napoleon too well to build anything on a mere probability. Instead of four weeks, I was detained in Paris for quite half a year. On my departure from Vienna the Emperor had confided the direction of the Chancellery to my father, Prince Francis George von Metternich. Since Paris was at that time the centre of affairs, my absence from Vienna could only cause any alteration in the carrying on of my department if my representative in the office deviated from my own views. With my father there could be no question of this ; and, seeing that no injury to public business would be connected with my distance from the capital, I kept to my determination not to leave Napoleon before I had attained the true object of my journey to France. The sequence of this narrative will show that I gained my object.

In May, Napoleon conducted his wife to Brussels. The Emperor had invited me to accompany him to Cambrai, so that I was an eye-witness of the enthusiasm with which the young Empress was everywhere received by the people. At St.-Quentin, Napoleon particularly wished that I should be present at an audience to which he had invited the authorities of the place. 'I wish to show you,' said he, 'how I am wont to speak to these people.' I saw that the Emperor was anxious that I should perceive how many-sided was his administrative knowledge.

After our return from this journey, the festivities were continued which Paris had prepared for the new Empress. Chief of these was the ball that was given in honour of the marriage by Prince Schwarzenberg, and which terminated so fatally.

I busied myself with negotiations for the execution of some decrees in the last Peace, and brought them with ease to the solution we desired. Napoleon evidently wished to give us a proof of his good will; and it was my business to draw from this feeling some advantage in favour of certain affairs of detail committed to my care.

But notwithstanding this, the great interest which had brought me to Paris was supreme in my thoughts, and served as a guiding star in all my actions. A veil was spread over the future of Europe, which I longed to raise; to this end I must secure a freedom of action which would have been hampered by a closer intimacy with the conqueror.

Therefore I remained impenetrable to all the acts of attention which Napoleon knew how to heap on those from whom he desired some benefit. I did not withdraw from intercourse with the court: I had the freest access to it, of which, however, I only made use, in regard to the Empress Marie Louise, with the most careful reserve. In the subjoined notes * I

---

* I. *Conversation with Marie Louise at the Tuileries.*—About two months after his marriage, Napoleon asked me why I never went to see the Empress Marie Louise, except on her reception days, or on other occasions of more or less ceremony. I replied that I knew of no reason for acting differently; on the contrary, there were many reasons for acting as I had. If I went beyond the usual routine, I should give rise to idle talk: people would tax me with conniving at some intrigue; I should injure the Empress, and depart from my proper mission. 'Bah!' interrupted Napoleon, 'I wish you to see the Empress; go to her to-morrow morning, I will tell her to expect you.' The next morning I repaired to the Tuileries; I found Napoleon with

have communicated some details connected with this

the Empress. The conversation ran on ordinary topics, when Napoleon said to me, 'I wish the Empress to speak openly to you, and confide to you what she thinks of her position. You are her friend; she should have no secrets from you.' At the end of this speech Napoleon closed the door of the room, put the key in his pocket, and disappeared by another door. I enquired of the Empress what was the meaning of this scene: she addressed the same question to me. Seeing that she had not been prepared by Napoleon, I guessed that he wished to enable me to receive from the mouth of the Empress herself satisfactory ideas of her domestic relations, in order that I might give a favourable account to her father, the Emperor. The Empress was of the same opinion. We were together for more than an hour, then Napoleon came back smiling. 'Well,' said he to us, 'have you had a good talk? Has the Empress said much ill of me? Has she laughed or wept? I do not ask you to tell me. You two have secrets which do not concern a third person, even though that third person is the husband.'

We continued talking in the same tone of pleasant raillery, and I took my leave. On the following day Napoleon sought an opportunity of speaking to me. 'What did the Empress say to you yesterday,' said he. 'You said,' I replied, 'that our conversation should not be known to a third person: allow me to keep it a secret.' 'The Empress will have said,' interrupted Napoleon, 'that she is happy with me, that she has no complaint to make. I hope you will tell this to your Emperor, he will believe you sooner than anyone else.'

II. *Counsel to be given to the Empress Marie Louise.*—In the course of the summer of the year 1810, Napoleon detained me one day, after his levée at St.-Cloud. When we were alone, he said to me, in an embarrassed tone, that I could do him a service.

'It concerns the Empress,' said he. 'She is young, without experience, and she does not know the ways of this country, nor the character of the French. I have placed the Duchess of Montebello in attendance on her. She is all one could wish, but is sometimes thoughtless. Yesterday, for example, walking in the park with the Empress, she presented to her one of her cousins. The Empress spoke to him, which was wrong; if she allows young men, cousins and so forth, to be introduced to her, she will very soon become the prey of intriguers. Everyone in France has always some favour to ask. The Empress will be beset, and, without the power of doing good, she will be exposed to constant annoyance.' I said to Napoleon that I agreed with him, but could not understand why he had taken me into his confidence. 'It is,' said Napoleon, 'because I wish you to speak of this matter to the Empress.'

I expressed my surprise that he had not himself performed this duty. 'The advice,' said I, 'is good, it is wise, and the Empress is too right-minded not to appreciate it.' 'I prefer,' interrupted Napoleon, 'that you should undertake this commission. The Empress is young, she might think I was going to be a severe husband; you are her father's minister, and the which may serve to explain the character of Napoleon.*

During his conversations with me, which lasted sometimes for hours, the Emperor Napoleon spoke with great openness of his plans for government and organisation with respect to France, and only touched on the domain of politics for the purpose of historical elucidation.

One of his favourite schemes at this time was the idea of collecting all the archives of Europe, in Paris. There should be, so he said to me, a grand edifice, erected on the *Place* between the Military School and the *Invalides*, constructed entirely of stone and iron, so as to be fire-proof. This building should contain all the archives of the European States. On my remarking that he must begin by getting possession of the archives before he arranged for their reception, Napoleon answered in the most frank manner, 'Why should I not have them? Will not all the Powers hasten to send their archives to a place so perfectly safe? Without any doubt they will be inclined to do so in the double interests of safety and of science. Only think, yourself, of the immense advantages which history would derive from this! Of course, each State must have the right of placing its documents under the care of keepers of its archives, who would live close to their papers. It would be free to each one to keep legal copies of them. What an immense advantage it would be to avoid distances ; one would only have to take

friend of her childhood ; what you say will have more effect upon her than anything I could say.'

* The manuscript here breaks off suddenly. What follows is the text of the ' *clue to the explanation of my manner of thought and negotiation.*'

two or three steps across a corridor, to draw from the historical treasures of France, Austria, Rome, &c.'

‘ I could not restrain an incredulous smile, and begged him not to overlook the difficulties which this project would meet with from other States.

‘ Well,’ rejoined Napoleon, ‘ see what narrow ideas the statesmen of Europe have, and do not know how to get rid of! I shall carry out my project; the plans for the building are in preparation!’ And with that he took me into his study, where he showed me a plan of Paris, on which the edifice in question was drawn. According to the ground plan, this palace of the archives was to include eight inner courts.

Our other conversations on political questions bore the stamp of academical enquiries rather than the discussion of practical matters. On meeting again a man so richly gifted, it was most surprising to me to see what thoroughly erroneous ideas he had of England, her material resources and her moral character. He would not allow of contrary views, and sought the key to them in prejudices which he reprobated. That he would bring England to reason by means of the Continental blockade, this he regarded as a mathematical certainty. He knew the state of Germany exactly; and on the internal relations of Austria he expressed views which were far from being unsound.

However great the interest of learning the thoughts and views of this wonderful man on the most different subjects, this did not afford me any satisfactory hints in explanation of his plans for the immediate future. The victorious progress of the Russian arms in Turkey gave me, however, a favourable opportunity of sounding Napoleon on the Turkish question. In repeated conversations on this subject, ‘ Napoleon began to lift

the veil behind which his thoughts were concealed.
Amongst other things, he said that he should not
oppose the establishment of the Russians in the Danu-
bian Principalities, which, besides, were more Russian
than Turkish ; Erfurt prevented him from doing so.
But this Russian success will be the cause of an alliance
between France and Austria: a political alliance
grounded on common interests, far more important
than a mere family connection, such as now existed
between the two courts. An advance of the Russians
on the right bank of the Danube he would in no case
put up with, nor with a Russian protectorate over
Servia. Belgrade belongs to Austria. 'You must try
to take this place by stratagem, or get the Servians
themselves to give it up to you. Begin by using it as a
depot ; once there, they will not turn you out.'

In the month of September Napoleon first began to
let out his views in our conversations.

It was at the time that, in consequence of the choice
of the successor to the Swedish throne, and the constant
increase of the prohibitions against trade and pressure
on the Continental States, a tension in the relations
with Russia was everywhere apparent, and Napoleon's
thoughts regarding his future attitude to this Northern
Power began to take a definite shape, which crept out
in his conversations with me. .

He spoke of the anxieties and embarrassments which
the choice of the new Crown Prince of Sweden had
brought about. When I said that he must have foreseen the result, which I held to be more a Franco-Russian
than a Swedish-Russian complication—in fact, it must
have fallen in with his plans, for he could have prevented it, Napoleon assured me he had remained quite
neutral, and had allowed the nation to choose. A French

marshal on the throne of Gustavus Adolphus would, besides, have been the finest trick anyone could have played on England.

On September 20, under the pretext of the latest news from Turkey, Napoleon detained me in St.-Cloud. He expatiated on the possibility or probability of a peace between Turkey and Russia. Then he came again to speak of the elevation of the Prince of Ponte Corvo as successor to the Swedish throne.

'I had news,' said the Emperor, 'from St. Petersburg, which proved that this event was received there as a thing that must be; it did not work well, but it was taken in silence.' Then he went on: 'I consider the Swedish affair as a more or less distant motive for war with Russia. That it should not excite envy in the latter is impossible. I shall have war with Russia on grounds which lie beyond human possibilities, because they are rooted in the case itself.'

'The time will soon approach—and I am very far from hastening it either by my wishes or my deeds—when hostilities will be inevitable. What part will you play then? I speak to you of all these things not at all in an official manner, and still less with the intention of making a proposal to you, but simply as we talk over any circumstance foreign to both of us. On this occasion you must either unite with France or you must side with Russia, and in the latter case you would remain neutral. The course last named will lead you to nothing, nor would it be the means of raisingy ourself; and if you attempt a merely nominal neutrality, in order to join the strongest party after the battle, you will get small thanks from them and small profit for yourself out of such a course.'

'I consider,' continued Napoleon, 'that what now

constitutes the Illyrian provinces is the most important district for Austria. These provinces once your own, and Dalmatia, would give you all possible points of egress which you are now without. I have the feeling that I humiliate and oppress you as long as I have these provinces. You must feel the same. There is, too, an ever-increasing germ of jealousy and ill-feeling between you and France. Will you one day refuse to confer with me for the exchange of an equal portion of Galicia for these provinces? Whenever I find it necessary to make war with Russia, I should have a great and powerful ally in a King of Poland. I shall not need your provinces, and you too will find this combination not less useful to you.'

I remarked to the Emperor that I could only speak on this subject with the full understanding that everything I might say should be considered as coming from the lips of a cosmopolitan, and not from the Austrian minister.

I divided the matter into two questions—the re-establishment of a kingdom of Poland, and the exchange of a part of Galicia for the Illyrian provinces.

'The first question,' I said to his Majesty, 'is of a purely political nature. A kingdom of Poland is nothing more than the Duchy of Warsaw with another name and with the new boundaries for which it has striven ever since it was made. Whenever our Galician provinces are reduced in size more than they now are, our interest in the Polish question must surely diminish in the same proportion. But it seems to me impossible to approach a matter lightly which presents such many-sided political prospects, and would alter the position of the existing relations in Europe. The Illyrian provinces are most important to us from twenty points of view.

Galicia has advantages on its side, for which it would be difficult to compensate. The revenue offered by Illyria is trifling, and hardly comes up to that of Galicia; it has fewer men and less means of subsistence. Galicia has important boundary points for the common-monarchy. If ever the idea of such a combination is entertained by the Emperor, my master, the exchange can only take place under quite different topographical relations, and will meet with many and great difficulties.'

In a long statement, Napoleon then explained the advantages which Austria would obtain by regaining possession of the Illyrian provinces, and, on the other hand, the great danger of Galicia to Austria in case of a successful war with Russia, which should lead to the incorporation of the Polish-Russian provinces in a Duchy of Warsaw, and must give it a great importance among the Powers.

'As for the revenues,' continued the Emperor, 'you have one means of compensation—buy all the estates in Galicia: they supply the principal revenues of the country. It can never be a question of the Galicia of the first partition; nothing would be easier than to fix the military boundaries in the north of Hungary.'

'Everything that I say to you,' said the Emperor, 'is entirely in confidence. I do not wish that anyone should know of it but the Emperor and you. I have never spoken of it to Champagny. If the war with Russia is avoided, I shall be quite content; but in the contrary event, it is much better to look at the consequences beforehand. I always put the question very simply as to what concerns me, both to myself and to others. So, for example, I say to myself in the present case, If it suits Austria to join with France, then she

can make more use of the Illyrian provinces—irrespec-
tive of their administrative advantages—than of part of
Galicia, the provinces of which are a cause of envy
between the two Powers.   If Austria's system inclines
more to Russia, then Galicia stands quite in the first
rank politically, for it serves as a connecting link.   I
do not desire from you any active co-operation, because
I have made up my mind not again to join any coalition.
I have had enough of the trial I made of it in 1809.   I
should have made quite another war for you, if I had
been alone.   I have never reckoned much on the Russians, but they have at any rate taken the place of fifty
or sixty thousand Frenchmen, who would have treated
you to quite another sort of war from the Russians.'

' If I speak thus to you,' said Napoleon in concluding his interesting and candid conversation, ' it is because
I will not let slip the rare opportunity when a monarch
can converse with the Foreign Minister of another
Power, and offer a new point of view to another Government, without expecting an answer.   I do not expect
the least response to this, which I have wished to impart
to you before your departure.   The purchase of estates
in Galicia will be a sufficient proof of what the Emperor
Francis thinks on the matter.'

I left St.-Cloud with the consciousness that I had at
last obtained light.   The object of my stay in Paris
was attained.   I had an audience to take leave,   and
returned to Vienna, where I arrived before the middle
of October.

I found the Emperor Francis at Grätz in Styria.
On his departure from the capital, he left a request for
me to follow him to Grätz without loss of time.   I remained four-and-twenty hours in Vienna, to obtain from
my father information about a political incident which

had just taken place, and to which I shall return further on.

My report to the Emperor on the result of my observations in Paris consisted of the following remarks :—

'During the year 1811 the peace of the continent of Europe will not be destroyed by any fresh attack of Napoleon's.

'In the course of this year Napoleon will join his own forces, greatly strengthened, with those of his allies, in order to deal a great blow at Russia.

'Napoleon will begin the campaign in the spring of 1812.

'Therefore the Imperial government must employ the next year in improving the financial position in two ways: first, by lessening the quantity of paper-money ; next, in making important military improvements.

'The position to be taken by Austria in the year 1812 must be that of an armed neutrality. The fate of Napoleon's undertaking, in any case a very eccentric one, will give us the direction which we shall afterwards have to take. In a war between France and Russia, Austria must take a position on the flank which will ensure a decisive importance for her opinions during the war, and at the end of it.'

The Emperor shared these views, and they led us, by ways apparently indirect, to the main object always before us ; and through all the varied circumstances of the following year to that policy the courageous development of which, at the right moment, was crowned by such decisive results.

Napoleon deceived himself greatly. First in his false reckoning was the conviction that the Emperor of

Russia would either not fight with France, or give way at the first victory, which Napoleon had no doubt of gaining. This idea showed ignorance of the Russian monarch's character, and a disregard of the vast space at his command. By all this the Austrian cabinet was made aware of its duty, namely, to be prepared for anything that might happen.

The incident which I mentioned as having occurred before my return to Vienna was, that the Emperor Alexander had sent his Adjutant Count Schuwalow to Vienna with a proposal to confer with the Imperial cabinet about possible events. I found a plan made out for a treaty of alliance in case of a new war with France, which was given me by my father. The project was rejected, as one not applicable to the circumstances of the day, or at least not suited to the spirit of the times. I was bent on securing the free movement of Austria with foreign nations, and on the greatest possible resuscitation of her financial and military strength. Count Schuwalow at once returned to St. Petersburg, his mission being followed by no result.

I thought it also a prudential duty to set our position as clearly as possible before the Prussian cabinet. The Prussian state was in the deepest decadence. The personal relations between King Frederick William III., Minister Hardenberg, and some other men trusted by the King, and myself, during the time that I was Ambassador at Berlin, made it possible that my opinion would be favourably received at this court. I used the opportunity to place the true position of Austria and Prussia before them, and to advise the King to patience and the remedies which time and its vicissitudes would effect, with the moral certainty that the Emperor

Francis would stand by him as a firm friend. The King understood my words, and they led to a personal relation between the two monarchs which survived the storms that followed, and exercised a great influence, not only on the history of Prussia, but also of Europe.

Alexander, Emperor of Russia.

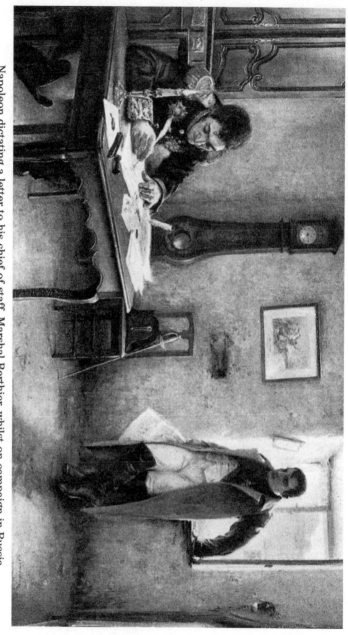

Napoleon dictating a letter to his chief of staff, Marshal Berthier, whilst on campaign in Russia.

CHAPTER VII.

BEFORE AND AFTER THE RUSSIAN CAMPAIGN.

(1811—1812.)

Principles of Finance—Finance Minister, Count Wallis—Minister of War, Count Bellegarde—Hungarian Diet—The Council of State—Academy of Arts—Dantzic, a place of importance for the Russian campaign—Armament—Armed neutrality of Austria—Meeting of the Emperor Francis with Napoleon at Dresden—Napoleon's ideas concerning the best form of Government in France—Napoleon's illusion and plan of the war—The elements of the Austrian military system—Confidential understanding between the Cabinets of Vienna and Berlin—The termination of the Russian campaign—Importance of the Austrian neutrality—The armed mediation—The Austrian auxiliary force in the Russian campaign—Warlike prospects for 1813—The consequences of the armed mediation—The return of Austria and Prussia to the basis of 1805—The German question—The King of Saxony places himself under the Austrian protection—General preparation for war—The Emperor Francis—The disposition of the people—The situation of Prussia—Feeling in France; in Germany; in Austria—Napoleon-haters—The armies drawn up in position—The moment arrives for the armed mediation of Austria.

HOWEVER bad was her condition, there seemed to be for Austria, in the domain of politics, a moment of repose; but I could not look forward to the duration of this pause beyond the year 1811. This year must be made use of by our country for unremitting attention to the most important tasks. First of these was the question of the state finances. The proper adjustment of these to the circumstances of the time would be a most laborious undertaking. The wars between 1792 and 1809 had exhausted the sources of public prosperity; the German part of the Empire was flooded with paper-money ; Hungary, by law, still maintained a metallic standard, but nevertheless paid her subsidies, small as they were, in paper only, without any regard to its depreciation. It was impossible to have recourse to credit, for if foreign countries had had sufficient confidence in the resources of the Empire to stand by it in the way of credit, in spite of its precarious position, this assistance would have been cut off from us by Napoleon, and by the ignorance which then reigned in the Continental states with respect to the system of credit.

The introduction, then, of a system of finance corresponding to this condition was not feasible, and attention must be equally paid to providing for the absolute necessities of the present, and the prospective demands of the future. To fulfil these important ends, the finance operation proposed by Count Wallis, the Minister of Finance, was very well suited. Count Wallis would have raised this to the dignity of a system made for perpetuity. But the Emperor and I thought of it only as of a bridge, leading from an untenable to a tenable condition, by the help of circumstances, the issue of which, however, was uncertain.

I must here mention one man, in whose knowledge of the situation, business dexterity, and devotion to the general good, the Emperor found a firm support, and I, assistance as enlightened as loyal, in the development of the fate of the Empire. This man was the then President of the Ministry of War, Count Bellegarde. With a thorough knowledge of military matters, familiar with my turn of mind, and quite agreeing with my political views, he was anxious not only to maintain the Imperial forces, but to strengthen them to the utmost, for every imaginable contingency, while avoiding everything that would attract attention. He alone was thoroughly acquainted with my views, and he knew how to raise himself, with me, above the illusions which assume the appearance of public opinion. He understood as well as I did the value of letting men talk.

The introduction of the new system of finance necessitated the holding of a Hungarian Diet, without the co-operation of which this would not be possible. After much opposition, the Hungarian states passed the requisite financial measures. As I shall afterwards have occasion to examine the state of Hungary more closely, I will in this place say nothing of its position at that time.

But what forced itself upon me was the imperative necessity of strengthening the central power. The Austrian monarchy is a composite whole, formed of separate districts which are historically or legally, from reasons of necessity or considerations of prudence, held together by having one common head. In a state like this, the idea of unity inseparable from the existence of an Empire requires to be matured and rightly defined, if it is not to become a mere personal union with all its attendant weaknesses: The existence of a moral body convoked to defend supreme sovereign power in the common head of the Empire, without at the same time restricting the exercise of the separate rights of the provinces, seemed to be the most appropriate means by which to assert the conception of Imperial unity.

A well-organised Council of State is considered by the impartial statesman to be such a body, and so it appeared to Prince Kaunitz. According to his proposal, the Empress Maria Theresa, in the year 1760, founded a Council of State of this kind. Sound as the idea was, the practical working of it was not free from defects. It seemed to me that one of the greatest of these mistakes was the admission of the heads of its different departments (ministers there were none) into the Council of State, and the direction of this Council by a High Chancellor. Under the government of the Emperor Joseph II., the Council of State had been in many ways mismanaged, and even hindered in its action by a cabinet government in imitation of Frederick II.'s system of government.

The Council of State came forward prominently again in the reign of the Emperor Francis; but soon after the death of Prince Kaunitz it fell actually into decay, a result caused chiefly by the setting aside of oral discussion, and the substitution of voting by papers. A later reorganisation was the work of some subordinate officials, who thought only of securing their own personal influence, so that the Emperor Francis was induced to dissolve it entirely in the year 1809. I devoted my whole attention to the creation of a new Council of State, in place of the old one. My intentions, and the proposals relative to them, aimed at associating with the Emperor a true Council of State, and, instead of councillors working singly, to form one common deliberative body; to give to the central power a more central spirit, so as to procure for the monarch, by a higher degree of tranquillity and security, greater facility for carrying on his own work. To the further course of this plan of organisation, which was to be carried on hand-in-hand with a revision of the institutions of the provincial states, I will return again.

During this interval of peace I was made Curator of the Academy of Fine Arts in Vienna, an unexpected and honourable appointment, which opened up to me an unfamiliar but most congenial sphere of activity, in which there was full scope for my strong consciousness

of duty, heightened as it was in this case by my inclination. I began my functions as Curator of the Academy,
and was anxious to infuse into the old statutes of the
institution (with the co-operation of Sonnenfels) fresh
strength and inner life, by reforms suited to the times;
and I endeavoured to invest it with outward brilliancy
by the reception of foreign notabilities as honorary
members.

In political matters the year 1811 passed as I had
foreseen. Napoleon advanced his forces as far as the
Duchy of Warsaw, and made Dantzig a *point d'appui* for
the supplies necessary for a great campaign. ' I have,'
he said to me, in the year 1812, ' in Dantzig secured for
myself a second Paris.' Russia was also on her side
preparing, and strove to end the war, in which she was
involved with the Porte, as quickly as possible, whilst
Napoleon was always endeavouring to add fresh fuel to
its flames. In outward appearance Austria seemed to
be in the enjoyment of profound peace, and was supposed to be exclusively occupied in healing the wounds
which the last war had inflicted on the Empire. Prussia
pined under the most unhappy depression, and endeavoured to stir up German feeling by means of the
Tugendbund; in South Germany, however, this had no
success. The armies of the States belonging to the
Rhenish Confederation prepared themselves to join the
French *Grande Armée*, in the ranks of which there were
already Spanish, Portuguese, and Italian contingents.
The Continental prohibitions against trade steadily
increased, and the granting of licences became a source
of wealth to the French finances. Napoleon's power
pressed heavily upon the whole Continent. It took the
direction of a system of incorporation carried out by
Imperial decrees. It was the eve of the catastrophe,

which to a quiet spectator had not, indeed, the feeling of a calm before the storm, but the sad aspect of a general humiliation of princes and people under the verdict of an inexorable fate.

The situation developed itself with the approach of the year 1812. The moment for Austria's declaration with regard to the forthcoming war between France and Russia had arrived. We declared for an armed neutrality. Napoleon demanded the contribution of an auxiliary army of thirty thousand men. The Emperor Francis granted this request, under the condition that the neutrality and inviolability of the Austrian territory should not be endangered by either of the belligerent Powers. All history has not recorded so strange a political situation, and it probably never will record a second example of the same kind. It was the result of circumstances, and a remarkable illustration of a period fantastic in every respect, and afflicted with every kind of abnormal condition. In the imposition of an auxiliary army from Austria Napoleon sought, not a material strengthening of his forces, for this did not seem to him to be necessary, but a moral guarantee for the restraint of the other part of the Austrian army within the boundaries of their own kingdom. The Emperor Alexander considered the closing of the Austrian territory as a useful defence for the southern provinces of the Russian Empire. Both sides acknowledged the neutrality of Austria, notwithstanding her contribution of an auxiliary army.

I was satisfied, for what I wished above all was to secure for Austria freedom in her political action when the moment came for decision with regard to the coming war.

When Napoleon, in the spring of 1812, went to

Dresden, to make from thence the last arrangements for the campaign against Russia, he expressed a wish to meet there the Emperor Francis. The Emperor complied with his wish, and set out for Dresden accompanied by the Empress and myself. The Empress Louisa was, it is well known, very bitter in her feeling against Napoleon. The manner of both Emperors was suited to their position, but cold. The daily contact into which I now came with Napoleon was a continuation of our intercourse at the time of my embassy to Paris, and my residence there in 1810. Our conversations sometimes lasted for hours, but we did not often touch upon politics. It was at this time that he explained to me his ideas on the best form of government for France. ' France,' he said to me, ' lends itself less to representative forms than many other countries. In France talent is common enough ; but it is only talent, there is nothing beneath it which resembles character, and still less principle. Everyone runs after applause—whether it comes from above or below, no matter : they want to be noticed and applauded. In the tribune they did nothing but make revolution, so I put them in order— I dissolved them. I put a gag on the *Corps Législatif*. Silence an assembly which, if it is anything, must be deliberative, and you discredit it. Therefore I had only to take the key from the door of the hall of assembly and put it in my pocket ; that shall be done with the *Corps Législatif*. Nobody will think any more about it, for its existence is already forgotten. I do not, however, desire absolute power : I wish for more than mere forms. I wish for one thing entirely for the public, order and utility. I would give a new organisation to the Senate and to the *Conseil d'Etat*. The first will replace the upper chamber, the second that of the Deputies. I shall continue to appoint senators to all the places. I shall have one-third of the *Conseil d'Etat* elected by triple lists, the rest I shall nominate. In this assembly the budget will be made, and the laws elaborated. In this way I shall have a real representation, for it will be entirely composed of men well accustomed to business. No mere tattlers, no *idéologues*, no false tinsel. Then France will be a well governed country, even under a *fainéant* prince, and such princes there will be. The manner in which they are brought up is sufficient to make that certain.'

I took the liberty of asking why he had not carried out his project. The Senate had without this already lost its credit, and the legislative bodies were reduced to a sphere of action which pleased no one; to which Napoleon answered :—

'Everything has its season; that for reform has not yet come. I must wait for two or three years, and who knows when the war will end which I am just beginning? That will come after the peace.'

On the whole, I received from our confidential intercourse in Dresden the impression that if Napoleon, on the one hand, did not deceive himself about the greatness of the undertaking, and looked on his success as the keystone of an edifice which hovered before his mind as a Carlovingian Empire under a Bonapartist dynasty; on the other hand, his undertaking depended on the terrible chances of war, about which he indulged in the most dangerous delusion.

As illustrating the reasons for my views, I will mention the following. Napoleon was convinced that the Russian army would open the campaign by crossing the boundaries of their own country. The conviction expressed by me that the Emperor Alexander would await the attack of the French army and baffle it by a retreat, Napoleon opposed both on strategical grounds, and from Alexander's manner of thought and action, with which he imagined himself to be perfectly acquainted. All which reasons told more in favour of my views than his.

When the reports from the army, drawn up in the Duchy of Warsaw ready for action, deprived him of all hope that the Emperor Alexander would take the initiative, he explained to me his plan for the war with Russia in the following words, which subsequent events have made memorable :—

'My enterprise is one of those of which the solution is to be found in patience. Victory will attend the most patient. I shall open the campaign by crossing the Niemen. It will be concluded at Smolensk and Minsk. There I shall stop. I shall fortify these two points, and occupy myself at Wilna, where the chief head-quarters will be during the next winter, with the organisation of Lithuania, which burns with impatience to be delivered from the yoke of Russia. I shall wait and see which of us tires first: I, of feeding my army at the expense of Russia; or Alexander, of sustaining my army at the expense of his country. Perhaps I myself may pass the most inclement months of the winter at Paris.'

To my question what he would do in case the Emperor Alexander did not vouchsafe to make peace because of the occupation of Lithuania, Napoleon answered:

' In that case I should in the following year advance quite to the centre of the Empire, and I shall be patient in 1813 as I shall have been in 1812 ! The affair, as I have told you, is a question of time.'

That Napoleon's plan for the campaign of 1812 was

exactly the one which he mentioned to me has become an historical fact; the same may be said of the motives which induced him to undertake the expedition to Moscow.

The following conversation between us may serve to throw yet more light on Napoleon's ideas :

'I begin to be a little perplexed,' he said to me on another occasion, ' about the perfection of your military system, which you have heard me describe as worthy to serve as a model, and which, to my great regret, I cannot myself adopt, because the military organisation of the two empires is not alike.   You have composed the auxiliary corps under the command of Prince Schwarzenberg of the *cadres* of twenty regiments.   Have you then forgotten in Austria that there is nothing in an army more valuable than these *cadres*; why did you not make up the corps of five or six regiments, which would have sufficed for the number required?'

' I am surprised,' I answered, ' that your Majesty addresses such a question to me.   The Imperial army, which a secret article of the Treaty of Vienna fixes at a maximum of 150,000 men, is now composed principally of *cadres*; for the Emperor, well aware of their value, has not, since the peace, diminished the number of regiments.   He now puts at your disposal a part of what you have left him.'

'That does not prevent this from being a mistake,' interrupted Napoleon.

If Napoleon was right in his remark, yet we, for our part, were not wrong.   Field-Marshal Count Bellegarde had composed the corps of Prince Schwarzenberg of more *cadres* than was necessary.   By the filling up of these *cadres* with soldiers, together with the army of observation stationed in Bohemia and Galicia to defend the neutrality, the whole forces of the Empire were ready for action, a measure which the Imperial Government could not have taken in any other way without exciting attention both at home and abroad.

The most confidential relations existed between the courts of Vienna and Berlin during the whole of Napoleon's campaign. Whether the course we pursued was better than the one which Freiherr von Stein and his political friends were never tired of urging upon King William III., I must leave to be decided by the actual events of the years 1813–1814. The results would certainly have been quite different if Austria had not taken so prudent an attitude in the last adventurous undertaking of the conqueror of the world. If we had listened to the urgent entreaties of the Prussian party, we should, without any means of defence, have seen Napoleon on the battle-fields of our own exhausted territories, instead of on the icy steppes of Russia. At any rate, Austria's course has not run counter to the ways of fate.

The campaign of 1812 was followed by consequences which even before it began I knew to be not only possible but most probable, on account of Napoleon's erroneous views. But I am free to confess that neither I nor anyone else imagined that Napoleon would attempt in the first campaign the task so difficult in itself, and which he had mentioned to me as to be put off till 1813, in case of the longer duration of the war. If Napoleon's whole enterprise was fantastic—the *va banque* of a gambler maddened by former gains—the marching on Moscow by the French army, which was prevented from fighting by the continual retreating of the enemy to the heights of Smolensk, was a mistake. The only explanation of this is to be found in Napoleon's firm conviction that the Russian monarch would not and could not expose the second, indeed the most beautiful, city of his Empire to the occupation of the enemy.

The continuance of Austria's neutral attitude after the result of the war with Russia, could have no other meaning but a confession of a want of strength in the Empire. I need not say that this want of strength was very evident to the Emperor and myself. The question which arose between his Majesty and myself was not on this ground, but referred to the direction we should take in changing our passive attitude into an active one. The King of Prussia, who had not been neutral in the Franco-Russian war, but had taken an active part by sending a small force to join the ranks of the French army, entered into an alliance with Russia after the dissolution of the French army. Our position was quite different from that of the Prussian court. Stein and the Prussian Particularists or abstract Germanists, together with the Russian cabinet, urged on Austria the immediate declaration of war against France. We did not allow ourselves to be disturbed in our quiet course, and referred the two newly-allied Powers to the decision which would be made known by the Emperor at the right moment. The bases which we wished to give to the political position of our Empire, called upon by the vicissitude of things to decide the fate of the world, are expressed in the following short statement, laid before me by the Emperor Francis, which requires neither amplification nor explanation :—

'The political position of the Imperial court is that of an armed neutrality. This position, if persevered in, would degrade the Austrian Power into a mere negation. This could be changed only by a rapid transi-

tion, or by a course of moderation which secures to the
Emperor free action in the future.   Rapid transition
would make Austria a member of the Northern alliance,
or lead to a union with France : while the latter would
be impossible, the former is open to us.   The transition
from neutrality to war lies in an armed mediation.'

The Emperor was in favour of the mediation.   The
most important considerations supported the moral and
political advantages of this attitude.

In relating my conversations with Napoleon in the
month of May 1812, I have already mentioned the circumstance that Prince Schwarzenberg's army of thirty
thousand men, consisted mostly of the *cadres* of the regiments.   This corps formed the extreme right wing of
the great French army.   Napoleon had not required
it to take part in the operations of the principal army
during the short campaign in the interior of Russia, for
reasons which have been already mentioned.   Prince
Schwarzenberg, whose army corps had been reinforced
by the Saxon contingent, had not, during the course of
the campaign received any orders from Napoleon.   He,
therefore, had sustained no losses worth mentioning.
After the retreat of the French army, Prince Schwarzenberg led his corps to the north-west frontier of Galicia, where it was opposed to the corps of Prince Joseph
Poniatowski, whose retreat had taken place in the same
direction.   Only a small portion of the Imperial army
had been stationed, at the beginning of the Franco-Russian war, to guard the neutral territory of the Empire
in Bohemia.   The greater part of the whole army was
either in Galicia or near by, as an auxiliary corps or
corps of observation.   Galicia could not be denuded of
troops so long as the Polish army in the southern part
of the Grand-Duchy of Warsaw was under arms.   There-

fore a rapid concentration of forces on the western frontier of the Empire was impossible, for in any case the
formation of an army corresponding to the strength of
the Empire, and adapted for a great war, would require
time.   We were convinced that Napoleon would use the
winter to begin a new campaign in the year 1813.   We
could not prevent him from doing this ; therefore it was
our duty to prepare to strike a decisive blow.   We kept
these circumstances in view, and the Cabinet avoided
giving any diplomatic explanations as to its course of
action in the immediate future.   That the part which
Austria must take in this future must be a most energetic one arose from the general situation of affairs and
the geographical position of our country.   When and
how this was to be done was the problem we had to
solve.   Nobody could doubt that the Emperor Francis
would strictly follow the voice of his conscience.   The
moment was too important for us to feel impelled to any
definite expression.   We kept back even our decision as
to the mediation, till we were satisfied that the right
moment had arrived.   After the end of the campaign in
Russia, our forces could be reinforced and collected, and
take up strategical positions, in a few months.   These
positions were to be taken up in Bohemia.   In our rear
we were hampered by the Polish force under Poniatowski.   The Imperial forces on the southern frontier
also received the necessary reinforcements.

In this position of affairs, my task was limited to
giving the Emperor a report on the situation in which
we should find ourselves in consequence of an armed
mediation.   Accustomed, in all situations, to put clearly
before me the aims in view—and to allow the necessary
time for their development—I arrived at the results expressed in the following short sentences :—

'The miscarrying of Napoleon's enterprise against Russia has altered Austria's position as well as that of the other Powers.'

'The final solution of the fate of Europe will exhibit itself by the Peace.'

'To bring this about is the true part and business of Austria.'

'In what way can Peace be established—a real Peace, not a mere truce in disguise, like all former treaties of Peace with the French Republic and with Napoleon?'

'Undoubtedly this can only be done by restricting the power of France within such limits as give hopes of a lasting peace and establish a balance of power among the chief States.' *

Napoleon's power, always striving to extend itself, was broken by the miscarriage of his last undertaking. Was it destroyed? No. The campaigns of 1813 and 1814, indeed, even the short campaign of 1815, proved the contrary. We did not doubt that Napoleon would not consider his power destroyed by the failure of the last campaign, and here our supposition differed from that of his open adversaries. They desired the immediate pursuit of the enemy. Of the practical considerations of whither and wherewith they did not think, and indeed considered it as loss of time to do so. My calmer judgment looked forward to a reasonable and successful termination, in comparison with which I thought nothing of a few lost months.

---

* The notion of political equilibrium has been much attacked since the General Peace (1814–1815), and the Imperial cabinet itself has been reproached with having taken up such a mistaken idea. The idea, however, apprehended in its true meaning, is not the less the only true one. Rest without equilibrium is a fallacy. Absolute equilibrium cannot, it is true, be found in politics, but only in a measure which offers the greatest possible guarantees.

The attitude of Austria as a mediatory armed power, said I to myself, harmonises with the geographical position of the empire, as well as with its forces, and will secure to the Emperor Francis the last word either in peace or war. Preparations to the greatest extent possible must be made for the carrying on of the war. By thus gaining time the part to be played by the Emperor will become more safe.

Two questions of the utmost importance were immediately presented to my mind. The one concerned the boundaries of Austria and Prussia. In the first place, this boundary must be fixed, as well in the view of the opening of a new campaign between France and the two allied Powers already at war with her as in the view of the contingency of peace without resuming the contest. If the precaution of a previous arrangement of the territories of the allied Powers were not taken, the war would become one of conquest, and, in case of a speedy peace, that peace would be wanting in its very first principles. We took our position with respect to both kingdoms, not on the basis of extension of territories, but on the restoration of their *status quo* in the year 1803 or 1805. The Emperor decided to leave the choice between these two years to the King of Prussia.

The other no less important question was that of the *quid faciendum* with all those territories which had formed the old German Empire, and which, after its dissolution, were divided into four parts, of which three belonged to Austria, Prussia, and the states forming the Confederation of the Rhine, but the fourth consisted of the great German provinces which were incorporated as departments in France. A German central political body no longer existed. First of all, we had to con·

sider: Should and could such a body be called into life?

It happened with this question as it is, has been, and will be with all important questions at all times. One may consider them from a calm and practical or from a passionate and hasty point of view. The Imperial cabinet took the first course. The German Empire of a thousand years was dissolved in 1805 and 1806, and indeed, strictly speaking, as much from the want of inward vitality as from external influences. If earlier defects had crippled the strength of the Empire, its continuance had become a sheer impossibility by the results of the Regensburg mediation in the year 1803. Not only had the German Empire been extinguished in the year 1805, but the German name had disappeared from the map.

The question whether a German central political body should be called into life could only be answered in the affirmative, for all imaginable moral and political reasons combined to support this decision. The problem remaining for the Imperial cabinet was therefore only how this was to be accomplished. To understand the disposition of the Imperial cabinet on this important point it is necessary to set clearly before us the state of things at that time,—a state which had, under the impressions of later years and the party strifes which issued from them, been essentially transformed, but which at the time when we write this (1852) again confirms the correctness of our decision at that time.

In deciding the point, 'How can a German state be again admitted into the European corporation of states?' we considered these questions :—

1. Can the old Holy Roman Empire of the German nation be called into life again?

This question we could only answer with a decided negative; for Germany (the name itself had only a geographical value) had lost the elements necessary to re-establish the old forms.

2. Could the fragments of the earlier Empire be gathered together into one united state?

We answered this question in the negative, on account of the following considerations :—

The idea of a state must rest on the basis of a united sovereignty, whether that of a personal sovereign or of the sovereignty of the people. The personal sovereign may reign over several countries different in their provincial laws and in their local internal administration. One sovereign people cannot rule over another. At that time we never thought of the latter; it was left to time to introduce it into German territory. The question then was, and could only be, of absolute sovereignty resting on an Emperor, and against this there arose insuperable difficulties.

The Confederation of the Rhine had assigned to the princes of the confederate states the sovereign rights which in the Holy Roman Empire belonged to the Emperor and the Empire. These states should have been forced to restore them to the head of the state; and the moral consequences of this constraint would have been but an addition to the fundamental evils of the former state of the empire, namely, to the unavoidable collisions between the sovereign head and the supremacy of the separate states.

Would the King of Prussia have admitted the subordination of his sovereignty to that of the German Emperor? and would the Emperor of Austria, on his part, have accommodated himself to such a pretension?

Of the re-establishment of a German Empire and a

united kingdom we gave up all idea, and considered only the formation of a German Confederation.

I thought that for the present the part of armed mediation did not require more than the establishment of these bases. There seemed to me to be a nearer prospect of war than of peace. I was convinced that the Powers had not, as they imagined in Berlin, an easy contest before them; but that Napoleon's efforts would be most vigorous—of this I was convinced, and therefore I exerted myself to develop the strength of our forces to the utmost. In this course lay salvation in the case of a war in which Austria would be called to strike the decisive blow. The means of attaining peace could only be discovered in the course of circumstances, and this required time, which to anticipate, I have always considered a fault.

A political interlude now took place. The King of Saxony, driven from his states by the united Russian and Prussian armies, put himself under the protection of Austria. He declared himself ready to join the Imperial court in its political action. We accepted his adhesion, and advised the king to await the course of events quietly at Prague.

Napoleon devoted the winter of 1812–1813 to preparations for the campaign. This was done in Prussia, whilst new forces were sent to the Russian army from the interior of the kingdom. Austria, on her part, collected her apparently exhausted forces, and led them to their places of assembly in Bohemia, and to the southern and western frontiers which had been moved forward within the old territory.

The result corresponded with the skilful preparations, which Count Bellegarde had made to ensure its attainment. In the states of the Confederation of the

Rhine new soldiers were levied to fill up the numerous gaps which the campaign in Russia had made in their contingents. The whole of Europe was in arms, and waited in anxious expectation for the approaching events.

Firm in his convictions and quiet in his conscience, the Emperor Francis stood in the midst of a commotion the result of which it was impossible to foresee. What made the Emperor so secure was the strength of his principles, and the consciousness that he rested on a faithful people and a courageous army; how strong these were the result has proved!

I should leave a gap in my picture if I did not say a word here on the feeling of the people in the different countries, and in different circles of society. With respect to the feeling of the people, very different ideas prevailed, according to the personal feeling and party spirit of the observer. I may describe the moral features of society, as it appeared to me, as follows:

There was a universal feeling of weariness and of the necessity of such a conclusion to the war, as would bring repose. The war had in its course of one-and-twenty years, covered with corpses many battle-fields, wasted whole kingdoms, overturned thrones, bowed beneath its yoke the republic of a hundred years, and as its final consequence seemed to have placed the fate of Europe in the hands of one man. This feeling, and the misery inseparable from it were universal, and were shared even by those whose opinions were generally in opposition. Conqueror and conquered were both weary and anxious for repose, in which to enjoy their conquests or to secure what remained to them; but the Prussian States formed a third and very different element in the general situation. The destinies of

Prussia differed from those of other states. If its dynasty had been destroyed by Napoleon, and replaced by another, it would so far have shared the fate of the French and Spanish Bourbons, the royal houses of Hanover, Hesse Cassel, Orange, and others. If, again, Napoleon had erased the name of Prussia from the map, the Prussian state would have shared the same fate as the German Empire, Holland, Piedmont, the States of the Church, and Tuscany. But Napoleon had ruled it otherwise with Prussia. The tyranny he exercised on it was unendurable, and he kept it in a state bordering on an impossible existence and final extinction.

France was just as tired of never-ending wars as the countries which, since the unsuccessful campaign of 1792, had had to bear the hardships of the actual battlefields, the devastation of their provinces, and the payment of the contributions. Napoleon had, however, given back to France itself the internal peace which she had lost, and the country was grateful for this benefit, whilst French patriotism rejoiced in the brilliant successes of his armies.

The results of the war had produced very different effects on the German Governments and the various German races. Mixed together and intermingled by the 'Mediatisation' of the year 1803, the feelings of the people of the various German races took quite different directions. The people of those German States whose territory had been enlarged by the Peace of Pressburg (1805) and the Peace of Vienna (1809) were contented with these and the protection of the conqueror of the world. North Germany, on the contrary, could not see any reason for satisfaction either in the union of the sea coasts with the French Empire, or in the establishment of German States under members of the Bonaparte family in the place of their own princes.

The decided feeling of the different populations of the Austrian Imperial states was for the preservation of peace. Austria had borne the burden of all the former wars except that of 1806, which had ended so unfortunately for Prussia; the inner strength of the Empire seemed to be exhausted, and the people to have lost all hope of regaining by force of arms what they had lost. In Austria, deserted since the peace of Basle (1795) and the later wars (1805 and 1809) by its German allies of the Confederation, the expression *German feeling* had no more meaning than a myth, especially in the high sense attached to it, since the catastrophe of Prussia and the northern German territories, by the upper strata of the populations of those countries.

A class not numerous but important from the position of the individuals composing it raised the banner of war in our country. This party only shared the feeling of hatred to the person of Napoleon with the people of the north of Germany, who called for freedom from the yoke of the conqueror of the world. They took the name of ' Napoleon-haters '; their voices died away in space, and their efforts would never have had, even if the party had been stronger, any effect on the mind of the Emperor Francis, or on the voice of my political conscience. The monarch would not suffer a repetition of those trials which the Empire had gone through after the campaigns of 1805 and 1809 ; and had he been willing, I should not have been ready to join him.

We pursued the plan known only to ourselves in seeming quiet and under the protection of secrecy. The extension of the armaments, and the grave preparations of every kind, were justified by the certainty, which increased every day, that Napoleon would commence a new campaign in Germany in 1813, and the whole people felt them to be measures necessary for the peace of Austria.

So passed the winter of 1812 to 1813. The belligerent powers, France and her allies on one side, Russia, Prussia, and Great Britain on the other, drew up their armies, in the beginning of spring, in strategic positions. From political as well as military considerations, we took up our position in Bohemia. The army collected there was placed under the command of Prince Schwarzenberg. The Emperor left it to me to fix the moment which I thought most suitable to announce to the belligerent Powers that Austria had given up her neutrality, and to invite them to recognise her armed mediation as the most fitting attitude.

Napoleon's victories at Lützen and Bautzen were the signs which told me that the hour had come.

Prince von Hardenberg, Chancellor of Prussia.

The Reichsfreiherr vom und zum Stein, Prussian administrator and reformer.

A letter from Metternich to Hardenberg, written in French on 2 September 1813.

CHAPTER VIII.

ON THE HISTORY OF THE ALLIANCES.

(1813—1814.)

Introduction—After the battle of Bautzen to the war manifesto of Austria—
Journey to Gitschin—Meeting with Nesselrode—Napoleon's attempt to
enter into direct negotiations with the two belligerent monarchs—Meeting of Metternich with the Emperor Alexander in Opocno—Invitation of
Bassano to an interview of Metternich with Napoleon in Dresden—Regulation of the institutions for the Austrian army—Metternich's departure
for Dresden—Famous conversation with Napoleon himself—Character
of Maret—Question of lengthening the truce—Second conversation of
Metternich with Napoleon in the Marcolini Garden—Convention of
June 30—Return to Gitschin—Conference in Prague—War manifesto—
War breaks out—Stipulations of Teplitz—Administration of the con-
quered German territory—The King of Saxony in Leipzig—Residence in
Frankfort—Residence in Freiburg and Basle—Residence in Langres—
Congress of Chatillon—Council of war in Bar-sur-Aube—Residence in
Dijon—Arrival in Paris—Entry of Louis XVIII. into Paris, and the
condition of France after the return of the Bourbons.

INTRODUCTION.

Since we intend the present work for publication, we feel
bound to say something on the object we have in view.
One of the most important epochs of our time was in-
disputably that in which the overthrow of the French
Empire and the return of the house of Bourbon to its
old inheritance took place.

Many particulars of this enormous revolution have
been given in various Memoirs. Its true history is not
yet written, and although we make no pretension to take
this severe task upon ourselves, we cannot banish the
feeling that the true history· of this epoch can never

be set forth with exactitude without the help of the materials given in the present work.

This conviction does not rest on any personal considerations; and to show on what it is founded we only need to mention the following circumstances.

History is built up of two distinct parts. One of these, the public or notorious part, consists of facts. The other part is that which is secret. It consists of the negotiations between the Courts, and includes the motives and causes of events. The first part, which we call secret, sooner or later loses this peculiarity. The official and confidential communications remain in the archives, and the day comes when they are picked up out of the dust.

This, however, cannot be the case with the history of the Alliance in the years 1813, 1814, and 1815.

By a coincidence which was not only singular at the time, but without example in the annals of history, the chief personages in the great drama found themselves together in the very same place. The Emperors of Austria and of Russia, the King of Prussia, and their three cabinets, were really never separated. The leader of the English cabinet had also generally been with his colleagues of Austria, Russia, and Prussia. At the Congress of Vienna most of the Princes who now form the German Confederation were also present at the negotiations. Since, therefore, the European potentates and their ministers were in the same place, the forms of diplomatic business had to adapt themselves to circumstances. The most difficult affairs, and the arrangements most complicated in their nature, were, so to speak, negotiated from one room to another; no sending of couriers, no written negotiations, no medium between the Courts: all these things, so necessary in ordinary times, had disappeared. Many a business which under any other circumstances would have required a long time for arrangement was concluded in the course of a forenoon. This state of things had two results: the first and the happiest was the success of the vast undertakings; the second, and it may be lamented, was this, that now the courts concerned are without any written accounts of the course of the most important negotiations.

Necessity always produces new forms. So it was with those observed by the cabinets during their meetings at the negotiations. The most important affairs were always discussed in confidential conversations between the three monarchs, as well as between the heads of the cabinets. Only when the matter had reached a certain stage of ripeness did the ministers come together for regular conferences, carried on with Protocols. A mere glance at these Protocols suffices to show that they contain no discussions. Where they are anything more than the mere formula of the point agreed upon, they give single statements, which show the shades of meaning in the opinions of the different persons who joined in them: shades which, however, never stood in the way of a general conclusion. Two new forms in diplomacy date from this time: that of giving Memoirs, as additions to the Protocols, and that of simple Protocols, with the form and value of proper conventions. It is to be wished that this mode had been retained, for it undoubtedly affords the greatest ease, and is on that very account the most suitable for the handling of great political affairs.

While asserting the fact that the diplomatic archives of the courts most concerned contain no documents relating to some of the most important negotiations of the years 1813, 1814, and 1815, we must except those of England and France at the time of the Vienna Congress. Lord Castlereagh and the Plenipotentiaries of England and France have constantly corresponded with their Governments.

It is therefore with the conviction that it will be otherwise almost impossible that the history of this extremely important period should be based on sure foundations, that we have determined to put together the present materials ; but we have also been influenced by another feeling, and this we will confess with the utmost candour.

Few monarchs have conferred more honour on their throne than the Emperor Francis. His people knew his value as a man. A true father to his subjects, uniting in himself all the virtues of private life, he was not honoured so much as he ought to have been by many of his contemporaries in regard to the qualities which distinguished him as a sovereign. Of pure morals and simple manners, averse to every kind of parade, he disdained even the distinctions which dazzle the crowd and often make Princes appear what they are not. In everything loving and seeking only the truth, firm in his principles and just in his opinions, this Monarch nevertheless often played what seemed to his contemporaries a subordinate part, exactly at those times when the extraordinary results were due only to his energy, his determination, and his virtues. The materials which we shall leave to an impartial posterity will not contradict this assertion.

It remains to us, however unwilling we may be, to say a word with regard to ourselves. The part which we have personally played in the events of our time has not been by our own choice, but imposed by a feeling of duty. Free from every ambition, but that of honestly fulfilling the tasks which, owing to a variety of circumstances, were laid upon us even from the very commencement of our ministry, we have never left the path which seemed to us to be the right one. Unmoved by the errors of our time—errors which always lead society to the abyss—we have had the happiness in a time full of dangers to serve the cause of peace and the welfare of nations, which never will be advanced by political revolutions.

In the reports and lampoons of the time, a certain significance has been always attached to our name, in which we have not been able to recognise ourselves. It belongs to posterity to judge us according to our deeds ; and in order to put it in a position to perform this important office, we have thought proper to give here the true grounds on which a right judgment can be formed.

At the moment when we write these lines (1829) the historian is not yet born who will describe the numerous events of the first ten years of the nineteenth century. Contemporaries cannot reasonably do more than collect materials for those who, at a subsequent period, will be called upon to write the true history of the past with that calmness and impartiality which are always wanting to those who have taken an active part in the events.

We ascribe, therefore, to our undertaking no other value than that of a collection of materials for the history of a certain portion of our time.

We have still to mention the plan of our work.

It is, as we said, not the history of the years 1813, 1814, and 1815 which we undertake to write, nor even regular Memoirs. We wish nothing more than to indicate, with unvarnished truth, the great causes and motives of the events. We desire to trace back known facts to their true causes, and to show the connecting links which are necessary for the right understanding of events. We shall be quite content if we can attain this object.

After the Battle of Bautzen till the Austrian War Manifesto, 1813.

On May 29th, about 4 o'clock in the afternoon, I received a courier from Dresden, who brought me the news of the loss of the battle at Bautzen. I went immediately to Laxenburg, where the Emperor was staying. I had made my choice. The point was this— to prevent Napoleon's onward march, and to remove all uncertainty as to the decision of the Emperor from the minds of the Emperor Alexander and King Frederick William. The Russian army was much demoralised; it had but one wish—to get back into its own territory. The Emperor Alexander had indeed resolved to carry on the war; but the will of the army might at last have got the better of his intentions. The Allied armies had decided to retreat towards Silesia. This manœuvre, well-planned from a military point of view, clearly showed the intention of the Emperor Alexander, who desired to drive Austria into a corner and oblige her to join the Alliance. If Austria showed that she was not inclined to take part in the war against Napoleon, this would give the Russian monarch the excuse to cross the Warta, and conclude the war.

The head-quarters of Prince Schwarzenberg were then in Prague, while his army was beginning to assemble round that city : the advanced posts occupied the districts of Saaz and Leitmeritz. Count Bubna had arrived at Napoleon's head-quarters.

I was convinced that if we joined in the war without having assembled sufficient forces to be able to keep the field, independently of the ill-organised and demoralised Russian army, and of the Prussian army, which existed only in name, everything would be staked upon the loss of one single battle. It was necessary, therefore, to prevent Napoleon from carrying out his usual system of leaving an army of observation before the Allied armies, and himself turning to Bohemia to deal a great blow at us, the effect of which it would be impossible to foresee in the present depressed state of the great majority of our men.

I proposed to the Emperor that he should go in a few days to a point almost exactly between Dresden and the head-quarters of the Allied monarchs. We looked out on the map for such a place, and Gitschin seemed to us the right spot. His Majesty decided to start the next day but one, while I immediately despatched couriers to Dresden and Silesia. The first conveyed instructions to Count Bubna to press on Napoleon the acceptation of the mediation of Austria, which had been offered to him. The other carried the news that the Emperor would shortly join the army. It seemed to me that these measures, or rather the mere fact of the Emperor's arrival at head-quarters, must exercise a decisive effect; and it was so.

The Emperor left Vienna with a very small retinue on June 1, at five o'clock in the morning. The day after, near Czaslau, we met Count Nesselrode, who had been sent by the Emperor Alexander in order to urge Austria to a rapid decision. He brought me a copy of the truce concluded at Poischewitz.

The Emperor Francis despatched Count Nesselrode with the following short instructions :—' Go back, and tell the Emperor, your master, and the King of Prussia, that you met me on my way to the head-quarters of my army in Bohemia. I beg the Emperor to choose a point on the frontiers of Bohemia and Silesia, to which I can send my Minister for Foreign Affairs, in order to make him fully acquainted with my decision.'

Through Count Bubna proposals of mediation had been sent to Dresden. Napoleon, in the hope of being again able to beat the Russo-Prussian army, and reckoning on the effect which a fresh defeat must produce on the two monarchs and their armies, as well as on Austria, had received the proposals of our Ambassador coldly and proudly. It was to be expected, therefore, that after the victory of Bautzen he would be more inclined to enter into negotiations ; and this was actually the case when he, according to his usual system, put himself into direct communication with the Allied monarchs.

Adjutant Flahault was despatched to the spot as Commissary of Demarcation; and Napoleon could count on his implicit devotion. He had flattered himself that he could influence the Emperor Alexander both by the choice of the negotiator (Caulaincourt) and by the power which he imagined he continued to exercise over the mind of this monarch. He deceived himself. The attempt had no other result but to let the monarchs perceive that Napoleon was striving once more to strengthen his tottering position by means of deceitful negotiations, in which he sought only to prevent the formation of a Quadruple Alliance, and gain the necessary time to replace the men he had lost by the forced marches of his army, and by the battles of Lützen and Bautzen. The Emperor Alexander and King Frederick William informed the Emperor Francis of their firm determination not to entertain the proposals for a negotiation ; at the same time they expressed to his Majesty their thorough confidence in his loyalty and enlightened principles.

On June 3, we reached Gitschin. I at once acquainted the Duke of Bassano of the arrival of the Emperor at head-quarters. At the same time I demanded a personal interview, to inform him that his Majesty had quite determined to give the proposals for a mediation the necessary authority. I was convinced that the answer of the French minister would be an evasive one ; and this was the case. I, however, needed such a refusal as a suitable pretext for a meeting with the Emperor Alexander, which I begged for on the very same day that I received the answer from Bassano. Opocno was the place chosen for the rendezvous ; I had chosen it on account of its proximity to the frontier, and being so retired a spot. In order not to be there at the same time, the Emperor Francis pretended to have business in Gitschin. June 16 I started, and arrived the following day at Opocno, where I found the Emperor Alexander, who had already been there for some hours. The Grand-Duchess Katharine, the Emperor Alexander's sister, who at this time was staying in Prague, had also arrived. In attendance on the Emperor Alexander was Count Nesselrode and several adjutants. Count Stadion and Herr von Lebzeltern, in consequence of the instructions they had received, had already repaired thither.

I went immediately to the Emperor Alexander. From the communication I had already had with Count Nesselrode in Czaslau, I was generally acquainted with that monarch's feelings both about the affairs and with

regard to myself. I had learned to know the Emperor
Alexander during the Berlin negotiations of 1805, and
at that time he showed me many attentions. By his
express desire I was to have gone to St. Petersburg as Ambassador in the year 1806. The relations which I had
with his ambassador in Paris in the years 1807 and 1808
confirmed his former inclination for me ; and not till
Count Romanzow went to Paris, in consequence of the
Erfurt conferences, was there any estrangement between
the Emperor Alexander and myself, when it arose from
the views of that minister being at variance with mine.
The marriage of the Archduchess Marie Louise, and the
absolutely necessary refusal of the Austrian Cabinet to
enter into a secret treaty with Russia in the year 1811,
did the rest. The Emperor Alexander did not allow of
any graduations in the behaviour of another, because he
knew none in his own political conduct, as he was always
going backwards and forwards from one extreme to
another, in the most opposite directions; he therefore
suspected me of being altogether on the side of France,
and of nourishing great prejudices against Russia. At
this first meeting, then, I had to be prepared to combat
the personal bias, always so powerful with the Emperor,
as well as all the difficulties presented by the political
and military attitude of Austria.

I went to meet the Emperor with the greatest
frankness. I did not at once attack his prejudices, but
made no secret of my conviction that the only sheet-
anchor for the Allies lay in an unbounded confidence in
that Power which, without a thorough knowledge of the
character of the Emperor Francis, as well as of the
principles and projects of his cabinet, might easily be
suspected. I assured him, at the same time, that
nothing could turn us aside from the position which we

had taken up for the good of Europe, whose preserver we desired to be.

The Emperor Alexander begged me not to doubt his confidence, but said that he could only see the ruin of the cause in every measure which did not there and then proclaim the true intention of Austria.

As I could not and would not give up the project in which alone I saw safety, I explained to the Emperor that I was ready to lay the whole plan before him, but must not raise any false hope that we could ever give it up, or even make any substantial change in it. I insisted on the absolute necessity of the mediation of Austria, the formal acknowledgment of which I desired to obtain from him.

'What will become of our cause?' asked the Emperor, 'if Napoleon accepts the mediation?'

'If he declines,' I answered, 'the truce will come to an end, and you will find us among the number of your allies; if he accepts, the negotiations will most certainly show Napoleon to be neither wise nor just, and then the result will be the same. In any case, we shall have gained the necessary time to bring our armies into such positions that we need not again fear a separate attack on any one of them, and from which we may ourselves take the offensive.'

This first conversation lasted over two hours, and we separated without coming to any conclusion. However, a short time afterwards, I had a proof that the Emperor could no longer shut out from himself the clear facts, though his natural distrust had not yet quite disappeared. The next day I succeeded in gaining him entirely over to the project which I had advised. I asked him to send an able officer to Prince Schwarzenberg, at head-quarters, which from this time were to be with the Emperor Francis. This officer should be commissioned to inform us of the condition and position of the Allied armies. At the same time, he was to be under the orders of the commander-in-chief, and to co-operate with him in the plan of operations with reference to the alternatives before mentioned.

The Emperor Alexander seemed exceedingly well pleased : he considered this to be a guarantee of our intentions. The good spirit which Count Nesselrode constantly showed in the management of his department, and the support given by Prince Wolkonski, one of the Emperor Alexander's staff, and Count Tolstoy, greatly facilitated the attainment of my object. Tolstoy, at that time, had the ear of his master, and indulged in a freedom of speech which subsequently brought him into disfavour. On June 20 I parted from the Emperor Alexander, who was quite pleased with our prospects, and able to look calmly at the chances for the future.

To enliven the Emperor Alexander's leisure, two cavalry regiments had been brought to Opocno, which were manœuvred by his Majesty during the two days for which the Emperor prolonged his stay after my departure

I went straight back to Gitschin, where I found a very pressing invitation from the Duke of Bassano to go to Dresden. Napoleon had heard of my meeting with the Emperor Alexander, and from that moment desired to arrange one for himself. This step, which I had foreseen, was a proof to me that Napoleon did not feel strong enough to break with us openly. I begged the Emperor to allow me to accept the invitation ; and immediately informed the Russo-Prussian cabinet assembled at Reichenbach, in Silesia, of the matter. I saw on their side much dejection. In my position, the strongest which ever a minister took, I was only anxious to convince the two cabinets that the future welfare of Europe depended on the line of conduct followed by Austria. Since, in the course of my official career, I have never derived support except from the resources of my country and the strength of mind and firm principles of the Emperor Francis, I was far from fearing the great responsibility heaped upon me by an attitude which has ended in raising our position, and in the triumph of the common cause.

The Emperor arranged with Prince Schwarzenberg and myself all that could accelerate the marching and arrival of our troops. His Majesty issued the most vigorous orders. Great as was this monarch's constant care for his provinces, such a consideration had now no place in his reckoning. His thoughts were fixed only on the great work that was laid upon him. It concerned the salvation of the world, and in this enormous benefit his people would find their compensation. All supplies which were likely to fall into the hands of the enemy were removed from the theatre of war; the most suitable places were fortified; the lines of Prague were closed, for this place was intended for a fortress. They began to lay *têtes de pont* on the Elbe and Moldau; enormous magazines were established for the use of the Austrian and Allied armies, which were to be summoned to Bohemia; a general conscription was begun of provisions and everything else that could be made useful in the war. The spirit of the people answered the expectations of the monarch; it rose as they gained confidence in the measures of the Government. The east and north part of Bohemia had now the appearance of a great camp.

I travelled from Gitschin on June 24, arrived the
next day at Dresden, and went to Count Bubna. Napoleon was just then absent from Dresden, and returned
in the evening of the day of my arrival. I therefore
did not receive Napoleon's invitation to go to him till
the next day, the 26th. His head-quarters were at the
Marcolini Garden, near the Elster meadows. He had
not the courage to live in the town; more than twenty
thousand men of his troops were assembled in Fried-
richstadt, and about this suburb.

The position of Napoleon with regard to the army
and the French people was at that time a very critical
one. The nation, formerly split up into several different
parties, had now only two—the party of the Revolu-
tionists and the party of the Bourbon Royalists. The
first of these consisted of the immense number of individuals whose fate was bound up with the Government,
or who relied on it for their positions, their professions,
or their property, which was mostly derived from the
nation. The first party lamented the precarious position in which Napoleon's love of conquest had placed
their interests; the latter, not yet daring to raise their
heads, waited with anxiety to see the result of the new
campaign, for which the nation had just made new and
enormous efforts.

The French army sighed for peace. The generals,
without exception, had little confidence in the issue of a
war which was more than unequal when the Russians
and Prussians entered into the new alliance. The hatred
of the German races could hardly be longer restrained by
the efforts of the Governments of the Confederation of
the Rhine, and when the attitude of this Government
itself began to be somewhat equivocal, Europe looked
all the more anxiously at Austria.

The appearance of the Austrian Minister of Foreign Affairs at Napoleon's head-quarters could, under such circumstances, only be regarded by the leaders of the French army as decisive in its results. I was received in Dresden with this feeling. It would be difficult to describe the expression of painful anxiety shown on the faces of the crowd of men in uniform, who were assembled in the waiting-rooms of the Emperor. The Prince of Neufchâtel (Berthier) said to me in a low voice, 'Do not forget that Europe requires peace, and especially France, which will have nothing but peace.' Not seeing myself called upon to answer this, I at once entered the Emperor's reception-room.

Napoleon waited for me, standing in the middle of the room with his sword at his side and his hat under his arm. He came up to me in a studied manner, and inquired after the health of the Emperor. His countenance then soon clouded over, and he spoke, standing in front of me, as follows:

'So you, *too*, want war; well, you shall have it. I have annihilated the Prussian army at Lützen; I have beaten the Russians at Bautzen; now you wish your turn to come. Be it so; the rendezvous shall be in Vienna. Men are incorrigible: experience is lost upon you. Three times have I replaced the Emperor Francis on his throne. I have promised always to live in peace with him; I have married his daughter. At the time I said to myself you are perpetrating a folly; but it was done, and to-day I repent of it!'

This introduction doubled my feeling of the strength of my position. I felt myself, at this crisis, the representative of all European society. If I may say so— Napoleon seemed to me small!

'Peace and war,' I answered, 'lie in your Majesty's

hands. The Emperor, my master, has duties to fulfil, before which all other considerations fall into the background. The fate of Europe, her future and yours, all lie in your hands. Between Europe and the aims you have hitherto pursued there is absolute contradiction. The world requires peace. In order to secure this peace, you must reduce your power within bounds compatible with the general tranquillity, or you will fall in the contest. To-day you can yet conclude peace ; to-morrow it may be too late. The Emperor, my master, in these negotiations is only guided by the voice of conscience ; it is for you, Sire, now to take counsel of yours.'

'Well now, what do they want me to do ?' said Napoleon, sharply ; 'do they want me to degrade myself? Never ! I shall know how to die ; but I shall not yield one handbreadth of soil. Your sovereigns, born to the throne, may be beaten twenty times, and still go back to their palaces ; that cannot I—the child of fortune ; my reign will not outlast the day when I have ceased to be strong, and therefore to be feared. I have committed one great fault in forgetting what this army has cost me—the most splendid army that ever existed. I may defy man, but not the elements ; the cold has ruined me. In one night I lost thirty thousand horses. I have lost everything, except honour and the consciousness of what I owe to a brave people who, after such enormous misfortunes, have given me fresh proofs of their devotion and their conviction that I alone can rule them. I have made up for the losses of the past year ; only look at the army, after the battles I have just won ! I will hold a review before you !'

'And it is that very army,' I answered, 'which desires peace !'

'Not the army,' interrupted Napoleon, hastily. 'No! my generals wish for peace. I have no more generals. The cold of Moscow has demoralised them. I have seen the boldest cry like children. They were physically and morally broken. A fortnight ago I might have concluded peace; to-day I can do so no longer. I have won two fights, I shall not conclude peace.'

'In all that your Majesty has just said to me,' I remarked, 'I see a fresh proof that Europe and your Majesty cannot come to an understanding. Your peace is never more than a truce. Misfortune, like success, hurries you to war. The moment has arrived when you and Europe both throw down the gauntlet; you will take it up—you and Europe; and it will not be Europe that will be defeated.'

'You think to conquer me by a coalition, then,' continued Napoleon; 'but how many are there of you Allies—four, five, six, twenty? The more you are, so much the better for me. I take up the challenge. But I can assure you,' he continued, with a forced laugh, 'that in next October we shall meet in Vienna; then it will be seen what has become of your good friends, the Russians and Prussians. Do you count on Germany? See what it did in the year 1809! To hold the people there in check, my soldiers are sufficient; and for the faith of the princes, my security is the fear they have of you. Declare your neutrality, and hold to it, then I will consent to the negotiations in Prague. Will you have an armed neutrality? Be it so! Send three hundred thousand men to Bohemia; the word of the Emperor is sufficient, that he will not make war against me, before the negotiation is ended.'

'The Emperor,' answered I, 'has offered the Powers

his mediation, not his neutrality. Russia and Prussia have accepted the mediation: it is for you to declare yourself to-day. If you will accept what I have just proposed, we will fix a time for the duration of the negotiations. If you refuse it, the Emperor, my gracious master, will consider himself free to make what decisions and take up what attitude he chooses. The situation is critical: the army must live; very soon there will be two hundred and fifty thousand men in Bohemia; they may stay there a few weeks, but they cannot remain for months in quarters.'

Here Napoleon again interrupted me, to go into a long digression on the possible strength of our army. According to his calculation, we could at the most send seventy-five thousand men to take the field in Bohemia. He based these calculations on the normal condition of the population of the country, on the supposed losses in the last wars, and on our rules for conscription. I expressed my astonishment at the incorrectness of the information he had obtained, when it would have been so easy for him to obtain fuller and more correct statistics.

'I will pledge myself,' I declared to him, ' to give you an exact list of your battalions; and should your Majesty not be as well informed on the strength of the Austrian army?'

'I am so;' said Napoleon, 'I possess most minute information respecting the army, and am certain I do not deceive myself as to its effectiveness. M. de Narbonne,' he continued, 'sent a number of spies into the field, and his information includes the very drummers of your army—my head-quarters have done the same; but I know better than anyone the value to be placed on such information. My calculations rest on mathematical grounds, and are therefore reliable ; in fact, no one *has* more than he *can* have.' *

Napoleon took me into his study, and showed me the lists of our forces as they were daily sent to him. We examined this with great particularity, and almost regiment for regiment. Our discussion on this subject lasted more than an hour.

On returning into the reception-room, he did not speak again on political subjects, and I might have thought that he wished to draw my attention away from the object of my mission, if a former experience had not taught me that such digressions were natural to him. He spoke of the whole of his operations in Russia, and expatiated at length and with the pettiest details about his last return to France. It was clear to me from all this that he was constantly endeavouring to show that his defeat of 1812 was entirely owing to the time of year, and that his moral position in France had never been firmer than it was in consequence of this same event. 'It was a hard test,' he said to me, ' but I have stood it perfectly well.'

After I had listened to him for more than half an hour, I interrupted him with the remark, that in what he had just told me I saw strong proof of the necessity of putting an end to so uncertain a fate. 'Fortune,' I said, ' may play you false a second time, as it did in 1812. In ordinary times armies are formed of only a small part of the population, to-day it is the whole people that you have called to arms. Is not your present army anticipated by a generation? I have seen your soldiers : they are mere children.

* The number of Napoleon's illusions since the commencement of the last campaign, with respect to the forces of his adversaries, is a most remarkable circumstance, and one which can be corroborated by more than one proof.

Your Majesty has the feeling that you are absolutely necessary to the nation: but is not the nation also necessary to you? And if this juvenile army that you levied but yesterday should be swept away, what then?'

When Napoleon heard these words he was over-come with rage, he turned pale, and his features were distorted. 'You are no soldier,' said he, 'and you do not know what goes on in the mind of a soldier. I was brought up in the field, and a man such as I am does not concern himself much about the lives of a million of men.' * With this exclamation he threw his hat, which he had held in his hand, into the corner of the room. I remained quite quiet, leaning against the edge of a console between the two windows, and said, deeply moved by what I had just heard, 'Why have you chosen to say this to me within these four walls; open the doors, and let your words sound from one end of France to the other. The cause which I represent will not lose thereby.'

Napoleon recovered himself, and with calmer tones said to me the following words, no less remarkable than the former: 'The French cannot complain of me; to spare them, I have sacrificed the Germans and the Poles. I have lost in the campaign of Moscow three hundred thousand men, and there were not more than thirty thousand Frenchmen among them.'

'You forget, sire,' I exclaimed, 'that you are speaking to a German.'

Napoleon walked up and down the room, and at the second turn he picked up his hat from the floor. Then he began to speak of his marriage. 'So I have

---

* I do not dare to make use here of the much worse expressions employed by Napoleon.

perpetrated a very stupid piece of folly in marrying an
Archduchess of Austria.'

'Since your Majesty desires to know my opinion,'
I answered, 'I will candidly say that Napoleon the
conqueror made a mistake.'

'The Emperor Francis will then dethrone his daughter?'

'The Emperor,' I replied, 'knows nothing but his
duty, and he will fulfil it. Whatever the fate of his
daughter may be, the Emperor Francis is in the first
place a monarch, and the interests of his people will
always take the first place in his calculations.'

'Well,' interrupted Napoleon, 'what you say does
not astonish me : everything confirms my idea that I
have made an inexcusable mistake. When I married
an Archduchess I tried to weld the new with the old,
Gothic prejudices with the institutions of my century :
I deceived myself, and I, this day, feel the whole extent
of my error. It may cost me my throne, but I will
bury the world beneath its ruins.'

The conversation had lasted till half-past eight
o'clock in the evening. It was already quite dark. No
one had ventured to come into the room. Not one
pause of silence interrupted this animated discussion,
in which I can count no less than six moments in which
my words had the weight of a formal declaration of
war. I have no intention of reproducing here all that
Napoleon said during this long interview. I have only
dwelt upon the most striking points in it which bear
directly on the object of my mission. We wandered
far away from it twenty times ; * those who have known

* The account of his campaign of 1812 alone took up several hours of our
conversation ; many other things quite foreign to the object of my mission
occupied his attention for a long time.

Napoleon, and transacted business with him, will not be surprised at that.

When Napoleon dismissed me, his tone had become calm and quiet. I could no longer distinguish his features. He accompanied me to the door of the reception-room. Holding the handle of the folding-door, he said to me, ' We shall see one another again !'

' At your pleasure, Sire,' was my answer, ' but I have no hope of attaining the object of my mission.'

' Well, now,' said Napoleon, touching me on the shoulder, ' do you know what will happen? You will not make war on me?'

' You are lost, Sire,' I said, quickly ; ' I had the presentiment of it when I came ; now, in going, I have the certainty.'

In the anterooms I found the same generals whom I had seen on entering. They crowded round me to read in my face the impression of the nearly nine hours' conversation. I did not stop, and I do not think I satisfied their curiosity.

Berthier accompanied me to my carriage. He seized a moment when no one was near to ask me whether I had been satisfied with the Emperor. 'Yes,' I answered, ' he has explained everything to me ; it is all over with the man.'

I heard afterwards that the same evening, at bed-time, Napoleon said to some one about him, ' I have had a long conversation with Metternich. He held out bravely ; thirteen times did I throw him the gauntlet, and thirteen times did he pick it up. But the glove will remain in my hands at last.' I have every reason to believe that none of those about him were satisfied with this speech. Napoleon's most devoted courtiers

began to doubt his infallibility. In their eyes, as in the
eyes of Europe, his star began to pale.

One man only could not break away from the
greatest devotion and fascination which perhaps history
has ever portrayed : that man was Maret (Duke of Bassano), who continued to live in an ideal region which he
himself had made, and of which the genius of Napoleon
was the centre ; the world has very greatly to thank
him for its deliverance. At that time he was detested
in the army. The incomprehensible operation of Napoleon against Moscow had enabled him to assume a military position ; all the reports of the heads of the different *corps d'armée* which were cut off from direct communication with the Emperor were sent to him. The
help he was able to give them was not to be despised.
He disposed of all the material resources of Lithuania,
and the remains of those of the Grand-Duchy of Warsaw. It was less a question of fighting than of sustaining life; from this time Maret believed himself almighty,
and thought his position could only be made greater by
the genius of his leader. I had no difficulty in discovering this when I had a conversation with him the day
after my long interview with Napoleon. I found him
in my drawing-room at eight o'clock in the morning,
waiting for me. When I saw that he only thought of
paraphrasing Napoleon's words, I contented myself
with telling him how that I was about to send him an
official note with the proposal for the Austrian Mediation, and informed him that my time was precious,
my departure to Bohemia having been fixed for the
next day but one.

I had left the head-quarters at the moment when
our different army corps were busy assembling. The
flower of the Austrian army numbered, in arms of

all descriptions hardly . . . . . . men. I wished to ascertain a certain point which would greatly affect the issue of the war; my conversation with Napoleon himself had raised the doubt in my mind whether it would not be desirable to gain some weeks' delay, in order to bring our *ordre de bataille* to its greatest possible completeness. Before the night was over, I despatched a courier to Prince Schwarzenberg with the two following questions :—

'Would a prolongation of the armistice between the French and the Allies be useful for the purpose I have just hinted at ?'

'What would be the most useful and consequently the only allowable extreme length of such a prolongation ?'

I begged the Prince to give me an immediate and decisive answer, and allowed six-and-thirty hours for the return of the courier. The adjutant whom I had sent came back, in two-and-thirty hours, with a letter from Prince Schwarzenberg, containing only the few words, 'My army would in twenty days add to its strength seventy-five thousand men : I should consider the possibility of obtaining this extension a happy circumstance, the twenty-first day would be a burden to me.'

From this moment my efforts were all to obtain the twenty days. It was not an easy matter, for Napoleon must have been making very much the same calculation as ourselves. How were two suspicious monarchs to be brought to accept this delay : one of whom knew his very existence to be bound up in Austria's decision, and the other of whom was obliged to strike some great blow in order to keep his dissatisfied and beaten army in obedience; and how, finally, should the impossibility

—in which the Russo-Prussian army was placed—be overcome, of living in a province stripped of everything, and how were the wants of this army to be supplied from the resources of Bohemia and Moravia without our being exposed to the danger that Napoleon would terminate the whole affair by a sudden attack on Bohemia, or demand of us that we should come to the help of Saxony, which was still more exhausted than Silesia? I put these difficulties distinctly before me, and I sought and found the means to remove them.

The three days following the conversation with Napoleon I was in constant communication with the French Emperor, the Duke of Bassano, the marshals and the generals. In our conversations Napoleon did not again approach the object of my mission, but referred me to Bassano, who again declared himself without instructions, and recommended me to wait patiently; while the heads of the army expressed themselves more urgently and more anxiously in favour of peace.

In the evening of the last day of my stay in Dresden, I received from the Minister of Foreign Affairs a written *Projet d'arrangement*, which had nothing in common with my demands, and which, therefore, I immediately answered by saying that I should start from Dresden without delay.

I fixed my departure for seven o'clock the next morning, and ordered the post-horses for that hour. A few minutes before the time I received a note from Bassano, which only contained the intimation that the Emperor wished to speak with me before my departure, and that he would receive me at eight o'clock in my travelling dress.

I had the horses taken out of my travelling carriage, and gave notice that the time of my departure was postponed, and I repaired at the appointed hour to the Marcolini Garden, where I met Napoleon walking. Here a conversation took place which it is hardly possible to describe. Napoleon's first words were : 'So you are pretending to be offended—what for ?' I answered shortly that my duty required me not to lose useless time in Dresden.

Napoleon then went over the text of the *Projet d'arrangement*, which had been sent me by his minister, and concluded by rejecting it. 'Perhaps we shall understand one another better, you and I—come into my room, and let us come to some agreement.'

When we had got into his private room, Napoleon asked me whether there would be any objection to the presence of Bassano ; in a negotiation there should be a Protocol writer, and this part should be entrusted to his minister. He rang the bell and sent for the Duke of Bassano, who soon appeared.

We sat down at a little table, on which the minister had placed the necessary writing materials. 'Formulate the articles,' said Napoleon to me, 'as you wish them to be.'

I limited my demands to the following declarations, in a few words :—

1. The Emperor of the French accepts the armed mediation of the Emperor of Austria.

2. The Plenipotentiaries of the belligerent Powers will meet the mediating Court at a Conference to be held at Prague on the tenth of July.

3. The tenth of August shall be fixed as the last day of the negotiations.

4. All warlike operations to be discontinued till that day.

After this statement of my demands, Napoleon said :

'Put the articles upon paper; I will add my approval.'

Never, surely, was so great a business settled in so short a time!

After Bassano and I had signed the act, and Napoleon had confirmed and accepted it by countersigning it, he said to me : 'He who wills a thing must also will the means to bring it about. In respect of the fourth article only, there is a little difficulty to be removed. My truce with the Russians and Prussians ends in the middle of July; it must therefore be prolonged to the 10th of August, a day of ominous import. Can you take it on yourself to prolong the existing truce?'

I replied that I had no power to do this; but that I was prepared, on the part of the two allied monarchs, under the pressure of circumstances, to guarantee the prolongation of the truce; upon this condition, I expressed myself in the following terms:—

'In order to maintain the armed territorial neutrality, the Emperor Francis has prohibited the exportation of all provisions from Bohemia and Moravia since the campaign of 1813. The Russian and Prussian forces so closely concentrated in Upper Silesia cannot maintain their present position beyond the existing truce (July 20), unless the necessary help be granted to enable them to meet the prolongation. But we have just heard the declaration from your Majesty that " he who wills a thing must also will the means to bring it about." For the Emperor of Austria the means exist only and solely in the removal of the prohibition which applies to the exportation of provisions in Silesia as well as on the Saxon frontier. Will your Majesty give me the assurance that the removing of the prohibition on the Silesian, Bohemian, and Moravian frontiers will not be considered as a breach of the Austrian neutrality?'

'Without the least hesitation!' answered the Emperor.

An hour after this last conversation I left Dresden.

After my return to Gitschin (July 1) all necessary arrangements were made for the commissariat of the Russian and Prussian forces in Silesia, and for the reinforcement of our own forces in Bohemia, for which purpose it was necessary to include the army then on the Polish frontiers. At the same time Poniatowsky demanded a passage through the Austrian neutral territory, in the direction of Saxony. The Emperor granted this demand. I, for my part, made preparations for the meeting of the Plenipotentiaries of the belligerent Powers in Prague, under the mediation of Austria; and the Emperor left the head-quarters and went to Brandeis, to be near the place where the negotiations were to be carried on.

The Plenipotentiaries of Russia and Prussia made their appearance in Prague at the appointed hour. Count Narbonne, French Ambassador at the Imperial court, who had been appointed second Plenipotentiary to Napoleon, had also arrived punctually. The Duke of Vicenza (Caulaincourt), Napoleon's first Plenipotentiary, was the only one behind his time. When he appeared, after the hour appointed for opening the negotiations, he came up to me at once. On my request that he would hand me his credentials, he explained that he awaited their arrival, but was nevertheless ready to take part in the conferences. I answered him that I should not open the conference before the delivery of the credentials. He begged me not to insist upon this mere formality. I replied again, that I could not do this;

on the contrary, I considered it my duty to avoid every
meeting which could have the appearance of a conference till the arrival of the credentials of the French
Plenipotentiaries. 'The Emperor, your master,' I said to
him, ' knows too well the necessary formalities, to have
neglected to furnish his Plenipotentiaries with their credentials unintentionally.' Caulaincourt persisted that it
was not so, and could not be so. ' The Emperor would
not,' he said, ' have chosen me to carry out any under-
hand proceeding. He knows that I should never have
accepted a mission under such auspices.' I explained
again the firm determination of myself and the other
Plenipotentiaries not to enter on any conferences without the strict observation of diplomatic forms ; all the
less since there were still differences between the Allied
courts and Napoleon with regard to the kind of the
negotiations which they should adopt. Only a fortnight
remained open until August 10, which was fixed as the
last day for the negotiations. They passed without the
letters for the French Plenipotentiaries arriving, and
therefore without any approach to the subjects about
which the negotiation was to have been held.

I had the passports prepared for Count Narbonne
in his capacity of Ambassador at the Imperial court, and
I put the finishing touch to the Emperor's war manifesto. These documents I despatched as the clock
struck twelve on the night of August 10. Then I had
the beacons lighted, which had been prepared from
Prague to the Silesian frontier, as a sign of the breach
of the negotiations, and the right of the Allied armies
to cross the Silesian frontier.

In the course of the morning of August 12 a courier
from Dresden arrived at Prague, who brought the letters to the French Plenipotentiaries. The Duke of

Vicenza and Count Narbonne then came to me. I told them it would be no longer possible to make use of these letters; the die was cast, and the fate of Europe was once more left to the decision of arms.

But this time the cards were mixed differently, and events proved that fortune and chance had their limits.

Stipulations of Teplitz

The attitude to be taken by Austria was clearly shown when the last prospect of a peaceful understanding between the Powers vanished. The mediation, which was like a bridge from one bank of a stream to the other,—whether the bank to be attained was peace or war,—was at an end, and that not by the fault of the mediating Power, nor of the Powers at war with Napoleon. Our proper place was, therefore, on the side of the Allies. To take this position rightly the basis of an enlarged alliance must be first arranged.

I will here give in a few words the views and feelings which the Emperor and I, in the most perfect harmony, laid down as invariable rules for our guidance in the immediate as well as the more remote future.

The object we must keep before us was the re-establishment of a state of peace, firmly based on the principles of order. As the means to attain this, I pointed out to the Emperor :—

1. The removal of the idea of conquest from the Alliance by the return of France, Austria, and Prussia to their former territorial limits.

2. The consideration of the international differences between consummated conquests and *via facti* incorporations of territory, without formal renunciation by their former possessors in favour of the conqueror. The

last-named must be immediately and unconditionally restored to their former possessors, whilst the first must, as countries delivered from the dominion of France by the Allied Powers, be considered common property, and reserved for the future disposal of those Powers.

The countries which were included in the category of *via facti* incorporations were:

a) The possessions of the House of Hanover;
b) That part of the States of the Church not mentioned in the Peace of Tolentino;
c) The possessions of the King of Sardinia on the continent;
d) The possessions of the House of Orange in Germany; and,
e) The possessions of the Electorate of Hesse.

3. The adjournment of all negotiations regarding the disposal of the countries which would form the common property of the Alliance till peace is concluded; and the reference of their final destination to a European Congress to be held after the Peace.

The three measures just named, besides their own innate value, presented the incalculable advantage of preserving the great enterprise from discord amongst the Allies.

With these we considered another object of the highest importance: the question of *quid faciendum* with the German territories. The points already elsewhere mentioned, which arose between the Emperor and myself on the question, determined us to give up the idea of a restoration of the old Empire, and to keep to the form of a Confederation.

That this determination would meet with opponents from different and quite opposite quarters was to be expected, and we did not deceive ourselves in the matter. We were well aware that many desires for conquest would have to be checked, many individual interests would have to be restrained. All considerations of this kind were subordinate to the aim and intention of the Emperor Francis, to secure to Europe and his own Empire the blessings of political peace for as many years as possible. Party spirit was not to be considered in an undertaking of this magnitude, and we did not concern ourselves about it.

After the battle of Lützen, the King of Saxony had, in consequence of Napoleon's threat of dethroning him, broken off his alliance with Austria, and returned from Prague to Dresden. If this step, which was explained by the condition of Saxony, cost the King half of his country, the other half owed its existence as an independent state to the monarch so richly endowed with virtue, but so hardly pressed by destiny; and at any rate it was only Austria who could complain of the breach of faith.

After the campaign of 1812, so unfortunate for Napoleon and his allies, the King of Bavaria took steps to obtain an understanding with Austria. We entered into this, not only for the sake of the reinforcements of our armies which would result to the Alliance from the accession of Bavaria in case of a continuation of the war, but also to secure our plan for the establishment of a German Confederation.

After the dissolution of the Congress of Prague (which had never been a living power), the Monarchs of Austria, Russia, and Prussia, with the leaders of their cabinets, met at Teplitz, where Field-Marshal Prince Schwarzenberg had his head-quarters. Negotiations as to the establishment and securing of fixed bases for the

Quadruple Alliance, and for the conduct of the war, were the tasks of the Allied cabinets. We pointed out, as the foundation, as far as we were concerned, the three points alluded to above, as well as the *conditio sine quâ non* of Austria joining the Alliance. For the greatest possible security of the military operations, we demanded further the union of the forces of the three continental Powers under the command of Field-Marshal Prince Schwarzenberg, and the division of the operations of the war into campaigns, with definite objects.

We appointed for the first campaign the time from the commencement of the war to the arrival of the united armies at the Rhine, where the three monarchs, with their cabinets and chief generals, would have to arrange the beginning and limitation of a new campaign. According to my conviction, we could not ask more, neither could it be less. The result proved that I was right. The elements of which the three Allied armies consisted were essentially different.

The Austrian army burned with a passionate desire to revenge the numerous defeats which they had sustained in the course of the long wars of the Revolution. But accustomed always to obedience and strict discipline, they waited in patience till the order should reach them.

Two feelings appeared in the Russian army which, though they arose from the same source, differed much in their effects. It was filled with a proud consciousness (which, with the Russians, easily degenerates into swagger) founded on the campaign of 1812, and a decided antipathy to seek new battles in distant countries, when they saw an easy and certain conquest close at hand, and that Poland could be brought beneath the sceptre of their Emperor, without their requiring to make any further sacrifices. It is more than probable that Marshal Kutusow, if he had been still alive, would have opposed in the most determined manner his master's order to cross the Oder.

The Prussian army only thought of taking revenge for a long and unsupportable pressure. This army, hastily collected from thoroughly national elements, long prepared and instructed by the *Tugendbund*, contained many battalions of fanatic volunteers,—fanatic as so many of the students and professors, literati and poets were at that time,—and burned with a desire to break forth at once into a war of extermination.

In this picture the portraits of the Princes and their generals must not be omitted.

The Emperor Francis, ripened by nature in the school of experience, ever dispassionate in his conclusions, never withholding a calm judgment, always acknowledged and respected the reasons for and against everything: holding his army well in hand, this monarch was always raised above inferior ends and the play of passion.

The Emperor of Russia was animated by a noble ambition, but he well knew that he did not possess the qualities necessary for a commander-in-chief. Determined, on the one hand, to carry out the great work of restoration, but full of respect for the feeling of his people and his army, which he knew not to be inclined for the enterprise, he was most anxious to secure success by rapid and decisive operations.

The King of Prussia, calm in the midst of a highly excited people, and by nature little inclined to believe in easily gained victories, even where his army thought them certain, was a severe critic of all plans (without himself bringing forward any) for the intended operations.

But if there were essential differences between the characters of the monarchs, those between the commanders of the three armies were no less evident.

The chief qualities requisite for a great general were as obviously possessed by Prince Schwarzenberg as they were wanting in General Barclay de Tolly.

General Blücher, was a man of overflowing courage and energy, but impartial history will deny him many other qualities, without which a general cannot inspire lasting confidence. He was, however, the true representative of the national spirit of the time, and the King could not have given his army a better head.

Behind the scenes moved two very different men. General Jomini had deserted the flag of the French army, and had just enlisted under that of Russia. General Moreau had been summoned by the Emperor Alexander, and had reached him at Prague. Mistrusting his own military talent, this monarch had formed of these men a sort of secret council, and indulged the idea that with their help he could take upon himself the chief command of the Allied armies. This plan was, however, soon abandoned.

The Emperor of Austria urged that the chief command should be given to Field-Marshal Prince Schwarzenberg, and the Emperor Alexander gave his consent.

The ill-timed attack on Dresden was made at the request of the Emperor Alexander, against the wish of the Commander-in-Chief. The great head-quarters were removed from Teplitz to Komotau, and the Allied armies crossed the Saxon frontier. The Emperor Alexander and the King of Prussia followed this operation; the Emperor Francis, who was opposed to it, remained at Teplitz.

A few days after the frontier was crossed by the Allied army, I received an urgent request from the Emperor of Russia that I would go to him. This I did, and met the Emperor in Saxon Altenburg.

The Emperor declared to me that affairs could not go on longer as they were, and that a new arrangement must be made in place of that agreed on at Teplitz. To my question, what change was to be made, the Emperor replied that he had decided to entrust the conduct of the war to General Moreau. He did not, however, conceal from himself that General Moreau, being a Frenchman, would not obtain the confidence of the Allied armies; that he, the Emperor, therefore, would take the title of Generalissimo, but that, knowing his own want of the necessary qualities, he would always follow the advice of the general, whom he would always keep at his side as his lieutenant. The appointment of General Moreau, the Emperor thought, would soon be justified in the eyes of the army by new successes; and the very difficulty which was thought to exclude him from the position intended for him, would in itself have a great effect upon the French army. He was certain that the mere name of Moreau, at the head of the Allies, would have a magical effect upon the enemy's army.

I at once declared that if his Imperial Majesty meant to insist on this arrangement, the Emperor, my master, would withdraw from the Alliance. With equal decision I withstood the expectations which the Emperor Alexander connected with the appearance of General Moreau in the ranks of the Allies, for, according to my sincere convictions—convictions, too, grounded on an intimate knowledge of the French character—the effect would be the very opposite, and would be seen only in the increased animosity of the French army.

After a long pause, during which he seemed lost in profound thought, the Emperor at last broke silence, saying, ' Well and good, we will postpone the question, but I make you responsible for all the mischief which may arise from it.'

Two days after this, General Moreau was mortally wounded by the side of the Emperor Alexander. When he met me the next day, he said to me, ' God has uttered His judgment: He was of your opinion ! '

There was one view which vehement politicians like Von Stein and others were never able to appreciate, but which was constantly before the Imperial cabinets : namely, that to secure the triumph of the Alliance so far as this was in the power of the leaders of the mighty undertaking, they had to consider not only the enemy, but also the Allies. If the agreement of members of an alliance upon a common object, and the sacrifices which it demands, is a problem difficult to be resolved in ordinary political alliances, this was preeminently the case in the impending war, in the waging of which Powers were leagued together whose positions, geographical and political, were as different from each other as were their actual relations to the common enemy. How profoundly different were the situations of England, of Russia, of Prussia, of Austria, and of the Princes of the Confederation of the Rhine, who owed all the growth of their power to the wars of Napoleon ! In league with these there was one element essentially different from all the others—the Swedish element, under Bernadotte, then Crown Prince, afterwards Charles John, King of Sweden.

It does not admit of a doubt that the Crown Prince had personal designs on the throne of France. Even if his operations in the campaigns of 1813 and 1814 did not furnish the actual proof of the existence of this pretension, the words spoken by him would be equivalent to a confession. When he perceived at Zerbst the peculiar courtesy of the Swedish soldiers to the French prisoners-of-war, it is reported that he said to the people about him : ' It is inconceivable with what gentleness the Swedish soldier tends the French prisoners ; what instinct !' And on another occasion, after the battle of Grossbeeren, when an adjutant of the Prussian General Bulow brought the news of victory to Bernadotte, as he was riding along the road, accompanied by General Pozzo di Borgo, who was acting as Russian Commissary, Bernadotte cried out enthusiastically : ' *La France au plus digne !* ' ' *Grands Dieux,*' answered Pozzo, ' *la France est à moi.*' The Crown Prince was silent.

An account of the military operations of the Allied armies does not fall in with the plan of this work, I will, therefore, touch upon these only in a summary way, remarking at the same time that the mysterious attitude of Napoleon, after the defeat, at Kulm, of the corps under command of Vandamme, which had forced its way into Bohemia, reversed the position of things, and that Prince Schwarzenberg availed himself of that favourable moment to carry out his first plan of operation, which culminated in the battle of Leipsic.* By

* On the 18th of October, 1813, at eleven o'clock in the morning, I went, in attendance on the three monarchs, to the place chosen by Prince Schwarzenberg as the most suitable point for himself and the monarchs to watch the battle ; and I did not leave this point of observation till the end of that bloody day, about six o'clock in the evening, when I returned with them. The monarchs required no report of the victory, for they were themselves spectators of it from a point commanding a view of the whole vast extent

the event, rightly designated by universal consent as the Battle of the Nations, the power of Napoleon beyond the frontiers of his own empire was crushed ; and in order to terminate the first campaign of the Allied Powers, nothing more was now required but to clear the German provinces between the Pleiss and the Rhine of the French forces.

Administration of the Conquered German Countries.

The revolutionary spirit which in 1807 had disguised itself under the cloak of Prussian patriotism, and afterwards in Teutonic colours, was, in the years 1812 and 1813, introduced into the councils of the Emperor of Russia by Baron Stein, General Gneisenau, and other Prussian and German fugitives. One need only look at some of the Russian proclamations in the campaign of 1812 to remove all doubt on this subject. The same spirit prevailed in the negotiations between Russia and Prussia in Kalisch. The immediate interests of the two Powers were, however, not left out of sight. They promised to help each other in the conquest of the Duchy of Warsaw for Russia, and of the Kingdom of Saxony for Prussia.

of the battle-field. The fate of this decisive day (not reckoning on accidents which may happen on any battle-field) was evident even by twelve o'clock at noon. The position taken by the French forces after the first morning hours was, and could only be, entirely a defensive one, for the purpose of covering their retreat over the river, which made a retreat to the west of Leipsic more difficult. An attack on Schönefeld, the farthest point on the outposts, and its capture by the Russian Guards, had no effect in deciding the event of the day, which had, as we before said, been certain for many hours. The arrangements of the Commander-in-Chief were therefore concerned only with the pursuit of the enemy, and the taking possession of the town of Leipsic on the following morning.

Knowing the religious feeling of the three monarchs, we may be sure that they ascribed the victory of the day to the Disposer of events, with truly thankful hearts; but that, on the news of the victory of October 18, they fell down on their knees, on the hill from which they had watched the battle, is only a poetic embellishment.

The conventions made on this subject between the two monarchs placed them afterwards in a false position in the carrying out of the great work of the political restoration of Europe, and they were the source of many and great difficulties between those two courts and that of Austria.

Von Stein was selected by the Emperor Alexander, after the retreat of Napoleon in 1812, to be the director of the future fate of Germany. His influence in the deliberations at Kalisch was very marked, and it made itself felt till the second Peace of Paris in 1815. But it was in Leipsic that the Emperor of Russia first introduced him to the Austrian Cabinet.

After the entrance of the Allies into that town, October 19, the Emperor Alexander sent for me on the 20th to inform me of the necessity of putting Von Stein at the head of the administration of the German countries already conquered or expected to be so. This administration had really become necessary, in consequence of the agreement, made in Teplitz, for the provisional destination of these conquests. As I had long known the perversity of Von Stein's character, I strongly protested against his being chosen. The Emperor Francis personally supported my endeavours, but they were ineffectual. The Emperor of Russia informed me at last that he had given his word to Stein, and that it was impossible to break it, without exposing himself to the reproach of great weakness. It was, therefore, necessary to yield the point. The committee of arrangement was appointed, under the presidency of Von Stein; but I acquainted the Russian monarch with my opinion of the deplorable consequences to Germany from the appointment of a man who was under the immediate guidance of the revolutionary party. Events proved that my prediction was well founded. The administration, of which the internal arrangement was made at Leipsic, became the support and engine of that party, and to its immediate influence may be chiefly ascribed the revolutionary turn˙ which the public spirit of Germany took at a later period. This administration was composed of the leaders of the popular party at that time, and this it was which organised the revolution that would certainly have broken out in Germany but for the vigorous efforts of the Allied courts for the safety of themselves and their peoples. It is sufficient to mention Jahn, Arndt, even Görres, and many others, to remove all doubt on the matter.

The King of Saxony in Leipsic.

At the entrance of the Allied monarchs into Leipsic (October 19, 1813), the King of Saxony stood at the window of his hotel to see them pass. None of the monarchs turned to look at him.

The three monarchs met to consider the fate of this Prince. We wished to appoint Prague as his place of residence for the present. The Emperor of Russia and the King of Prussia had already determined to send him to Berlin. We agreed that the monarchs should ·not see the King, and I was charged to announce his fate to him. I went to the King's palace, and was admitted without delay. The King awaited me standing in his reception-room, and received me with friendliness. I executed my mission with as much delicacy as possible. The King listened, not without emotion, but with an expression of thorough resignation. He said some words and tried to make me understand that his position was of such a kind that no other attitude had been possible

for him.   I answered that, in my capacity of leader of
the cabinet, I felt it to be my duty to point out to him
that all his misfortunes were the consequence of his first
mistake of refusing the hand we had stretched out to
save him and his country. ˙ The King offered me his
sword.   I explained to him that I did not consider myself authorised to receive it.

During our conversation the Queen of Saxony entered
the room.   When she heard the object of my visit, she
betrayed the greatest agitation.   She reproached me
bitterly that I myself had opposed Napoleon's cause,
which she called the cause of God.   I answered her
quietly that I had not come to the King to argue this
matter with her.   The King immediately departed for
Berlin and Freienwalde.

Residence in Frankfort.

Frankfort was, from its situation, the place where
the future operations had to be arranged.   Up to this
time the monarchs had only followed the movements of
the army after the battle of Leipsic.   The only diplomatic action between October 18 and November 6, the
day of the Emperor of Austria's arrival in Frankfort,
was the Peace which I signed at Fulda, on November 2,
with the King of Wurtemberg.   The Princes of the
Confederation of the Rhine had sent plenipotentiaries
in great haste to Frankfort, in order to join in the
conference with the Allies.   The united Cabinets appointed Plenipotentiaries for the business of signing the
different documents.   These Plenipotentiaries were, for
Austria Baron Binder, for Russia Herr von Anstett, and
for Prussia Baron von Humboldt.   They signed in one
day twenty-two treaties.

The great political question was to fix the course of

a new campaign.   Germany was evacuated : of French
military there were only the garrisons of some fortresses
on the Oder and the Elbe.   The Allied armies, everywhere victorious, were now still further reinforced by
the German contingents.   The object of the war of 1813
was attained—Napoleon was repulsed and driven back
over the Rhine.   What was to be done in the next year?
This was what we had to decide.

On the following points we were all agreed :—

1. To carry the war beyond the Rhine into the
interior of France.

2. By this proceeding to strike a blow at the very
existence of the Emperor Napoleon which might be
decisive in its consequences.

3. To wait to see what effect the misfortunes of the
two last campaigns and the invasion of the French territory would have on the mind of the nation ; further

4. It was resolved, at my suggestion, that if once
the heights of the Vosges and the Ardennes were occupied, a plan must be made for the military operations
which would amount to a third campaign, deciding the
future fate of France, and therefore also the triumph
of the Quadruple Alliance.   The most important motives
decided me to this course.   They will be seen more
clearly in the sketch I shall afterwards give of the
' Residence in Langres.'

But, before crossing the Rhine, some resolutions
must be taken on both moral and military grounds.   It
was not an easy undertaking.

The Emperor of Russia, prepossessed by revolutionary ideas, surrounded by men like Laharpe, Stein, and
Jomini, entertained plans which would have led the
world to ruin.   The Russian army remained quiet, and
thought its object gained.   If Marshal Kutusow had been

still living, it would not have left the Oder. The Prussian army ruled the cabinet; it thirsted only for revenge. Blücher and the Free Corps thought only of the destruction and plundering of Paris. The revolutionary seed, which had borne so much fruit in Prussia since 1808, grew and flourished on this extensive field. Men like Arndt, Jahn, and others, who distinguished themselves so deplorably, had all appointments in the army at Frankfort, or about the ministers.

The efforts of the Emperor of Austria were directed to good ends only; and the task fell on me, in these difficult circumstances, to clear the way for events, and prevent evil designs from neutralising the really good, and bringing about a situation which would only too easily have involved the future of society itself.

I proposed, in the first place, to issue a manifesto to the French people, in the name of the Allied monarchs, to enlighten the French nation on the motives and objects of the invasion.

Being thoroughly acquainted with the public feeling in France, I felt certain that in the appeal mention should be made of the Rhine, the Alps, and the Pyrenees as the natural boundaries of France, thus offering a bait which would be taken by all, and flattering the vanity instead of embittering the feelings of the nation. Intending to separate Napoleon still more from the nation, and at the same time to act on the mind of the army, I proposed further to join with the idea of natural boundaries the offer of an immediate negotiation. As the Emperor Francis sanctioned my intention, I laid it before their Majesties of Russia and Prussia. Both of them feared that Napoleon, trusting to the chances of the future, might by accepting the proposal with quick and energetic decision, put an end to the affair. I used all my powers of persuasion on the two monarchs to lead them to share my conviction that Napoleon would never voluntarily take such a decision. The substance of the proclamation was decided on, and it was left to me to fill up the details.

Baron St.-Aignan, the French Ambassador at the ducal court of Saxony, had been taken prisoner in Gotha, and brought to Bohemia by the troops of the Allies. I proposed to make amends for a proceeding so contrary to all international rights, and to take advantage of his being summoned to Frankfort, to let the Emperor Napoleon know of our projected plan. Baron St.-Aignan was summoned, and I had a long conversation with him, in the presence of Count Nesselrode and Lord Aberdeen, and we then allowed him to depart immediately for Paris. At the same time twenty thousand copies of the proclamation were printed and sent, by all possible means, across the Rhine and all over France. Afterwards I heard from the Prince of Neufchâtel that the first of the proclamations which was posted up in Paris was brought by Savary, then Minister of Police, to the Emperor Napoleon, who, on reading it, said: ' No one but Metternich can have concocted this document ; talking of the Rhine, the Alps, and the Pyrenees is a thorough piece of cunning. It could only enter into the head of a man who knows France as well as he does.'

Napoleon had made a proposal for the renewal of the negotiations for the conclusion of peace. On the side of Prussia, the feeling was decidedly against any such negotiations. The Emperor Alexander inclined to the opinion of the Austrian Cabinet, that the way should never be closed against peaceful tendencies, even in the hottest fight. The Emperor Francis believed in the sincerity of Napoleon's mood ; but I was convinced of the contrary. It seemed to me that an acceptable end of the war could not be intended by the man who had, as it were, burned his ships behind him; but I thought it the duty of the Powers at least to hear the conditions with which Napoleon was prepared to come forward.

The three courts answered the proposals of Napoleon with the calm consciousness of strength, and declared themselves ready for a meeting of deputies in Mannheim; but refused to listen to any hints for the suspension of warlike operations. My prediction that the idea of peace was far from Napoleon proved to be right. He never carried out the meeting in Mannheim.

The question was now to arrange the plans for the military operations, and this presented great difficulties.

Field-Marshal Prince Schwarzenberg proposed a general attack on three lines of operation: namely, the right wing of the great army, consisting of the Prussian forces, under the command of General Blücher, should cross the Rhine between Mayence and Cologne, advance towards the Netherlands, and take the direction to Lothringen and the slopes of the Ardennes. The centre of the army, composed of Austrian and Russian troops, should cross the Rhine between Mannheim and Basle, and lead the chief line of operations of the Austrian army through Switzerland. A corps of the latter, under the command of General Bubna, would have to march out of Italy by the Simplon Pass, to occupy La Vallée, to take Geneva and Lyons, and thus to form the extreme outer left wing.

The impatience of the Prussian army, and its wish to get to Paris as soon as possible, even if it went alone, decided Marshal Blücher to propose an operation directed towards Verdun, like the one which ended so unfortunately in 1792. Supported by the Russian and Austrian forces, he did not fear similar misfortunes, whilst this operation would really have brought him to Paris by the shortest route.

A subordinate circumstance, but one of the kind which had already so often influenced the Emperor of Russia, determined his Imperial Majesty to propose a modified plan, between those of the Austrian and Prussian generals. This proposal was grounded on the desire that the neutrality of Switzerland should be respected, and presupposed a general and simultaneous movement of the Allied armies, to cross the Rhine in several places between Altbreisach and Cologne. The secret of this plan was as follows :—

Laharpe, Jomini, and other Swiss revolutionaries, had urged vehemently on the Emperor Alexander what they called respect for Helvetian neutrality. Several considerations had led them to this wish. Laharpe and the Vaudois feared a return to the old order of things, as a consequence of which the new Cantons might lose their political existence. Whereas by preserving their political existence, they hoped to succeed in transforming the old Cantons into an entirely democratic system. Lastly, Laharpe and his friends wished to keep Switzerland, whatever might happen, open as an asylum for the revolutionaries of France, and of all other countries occupied, or which might be occupied, by the Allies. The Emperor of Russia had committed himself to them by certain engagements ; but they set other springs in motion to make their cause certain. They suggested the despatch of a deputation to Frankfort to require the confirmation of the neutrality. The Emperor of Russia, without giving any decided promises, such as he had given to some of his intimate friends, did not, however, fail to dismiss the deputation with a confident hope that the neutrality of Switzerland would not be violated. But there was another circumstance which had a much more decisive effect upon the attitude of the Emperor.

A lady, formerly governess of the Grand-Duchess Marie of Weimar, a Vaudois who had been sent by the Cantons to Frankfort to implore the support of her Imperial Highness, had been listened to by the Princess. The Emperor Alexander, on his side, had promised his sister that he would never allow the Allied armies to enter Switzerland. He even empowered her to mention this promise in a letter which the Grand-Duchess wrote to her former governess, and which the Grand-Duchess expressly allowed her to show in confidence to her friends at Lausanne.

Several days were lost in mere councils of war between the leaders of the different armies. Each of them defended his own plan of operation; and all rational arguments supported the plan of Field-Marshal Prince Schwarzenberg, which had the more to say for itself as the preliminary preparations, made by me in Switzerland, could leave us no doubt that the sound part of the Swiss people would give a good reception to the Austrian army, which was the only one that could enter Switzerland, and would welcome them as liberators. When the Emperor of Russia had lost all hope of bringing the Austrian and Prussian generals over to his plan, one evening about ten o'clock he sent to me Prince Demeter Wolkonski, chief of the staff, with an invitation to come to him without delay.

Introduced into the closet of his Imperial Majesty, I found the generals of the three armies assembled there. The Emperor at once began, and said to me

that the council of war, after fruitless endeavours to
agree about the plan of impending operations, had come
to the resolution of referring the decision to a third
person, and that his—the Emperor's—choice had fallen
upon me. Although not in doubt what I should do, I
nevertheless asked to be informed of the discussion
which had taken place. The Emperor then undertook
to explain to me the different plans of operation.

I began by insisting on the analogy of the views
of his Imperial Majesty with those of the Austrian
commander, and on the strong grounds which existed
for the choice of Switzerland as a basis of operation.
The Emperor, although he allowed me to unfold all the
military and political grounds which I brought forward
in the support of my advice, at last expressed himself
to this effect : that, although he did not deny the
cogency of my arguments, he could never agree to the
violation of the neutrality of Switzerland. I replied to
the Emperor that such a measure would as little fall in
with my views ; but the most important grounds permitted me to assume it as a certainty that whenever we
appeared on the soil of the Confederation we should be
received as friends and liberators. His Majesty replied
to me that special grounds and considerations, which
perhaps applied only to himself, would always restrain
him from exposing himself to the danger, or even the
possibility, of meeting with opposition from the Cantons.
Ultimately the Emperor consented that if we should
succeed in obtaining permission from the Swiss to make
use of the bridge at Basle, to this he would make no
objection. Upon this concession, I advanced a step
further, and, without rejecting it, I expressed my conviction that the permission to pass through the whole
territory of the Confederation would encounter no

more opposition than would the permission to cross the one bridge, by which the partisans of the pretended neutrality would consider it just as much violated. 1 concluded the discussion by deciding in favour of the plan of Prince Schwarzenberg, with due consideration for the wishes of his Majesty the Emperor Alexander, especially in paying all possible respect to the Swiss Confederation.

Residence in Freiburg and Basle.

During the negotiations in Frankfort I had taken every possible step to obtain permission for the entrance of the Imperial troops into Switzerland. Baron Lebzeltern was in Zurich at the *Bundesdirectorium,* Count Senfft in Berne. Prince Schwarzenberg had put himself into immediate communication with the military chiefs of the Swiss contingents. There could be no doubt that the army would be well received in Switzerland, and that at their first appearance the troops of the Republic would join them.

Since Marshal Blücher's plan of operations was set aside, the head-quarters of the Russian and Austrian army were removed to Brisgau.

Prince Schwarzenberg had hastened on several days before the departure of their Majesties, and fixed on Lörrach for their head-quarters. When I was in Frankfort, I received a letter from him, in which he informed me of the impossibility of his putting off crossing the Rhine beyond the end of the year, because the means were wanting to support the numerous forces drawn up from Schaffhausen to the heights of Freiburg. At the same time he let me know that, in concert with the Swiss generals, he had made arrangements to cross the Rhine from Schaffhausen to Basle at all the necessary points. I presented myself to take the orders of the Emperor, and set out without delay to Freiburg, authorised by his Majesty to make all arrangements for carrying out the operation with the commander-in-chief.

The Emperor of Russia had left Frankfort two days earlier, and was in Carlsruhe with the family of the Empress. I made my arrangements so that I had to pass this town at two o'clock in the morning. The Emperor Francis followed me five-and-twenty hours later. Immediately on my arrival in Freiburg, I found the last news required for the final arrangement of my diplomatic plan, which was designed to support the military plan of the field-marshal. The same night I sent to Baron Lebzeltern in Zurich a courier with the sketch of the official note, which was to be delivered to the Diet assembled in that town. Prince Schwarzenberg ordered the crossing of the Rhine; and on the arrival of the Emperor in Freiburg, I was so fortunate as to be able to inform him that the troops of the Confederation had joined those of his Majesty, and that the latter had everywhere met with the most favourable reception.

There still remained the difficulty of informing his Majesty the Emperor of Russia that the event had really been accomplished which he had pronounced to be impossible. The Emperor Francis instructed me to execute this commission on the following day, when the arrival of his ally was expected.

On December 22 the Emperor went to meet the Russian monarch two miles outside the town. I accompanied his Majesty. At the moment of the meeting of the two monarchs, the Emperor Alexander addressed me with the question whether there was any news. I replied that I could not answer his question till we had arrived at the hotel. The Emperor Francis accompanied the Emperor of Russia to his apartments, and then left him. The latter asked me to come into his private room: 'Your Majesty,' I said, 'has addressed a question to me which it was impossible for me to answer in the presence of so many persons. I am not yet certain how your Majesty will take what I have to tell you, even here between ourselves. The Austrian army crossed the Rhine, the night before last, at several points between Schaffhausen and Basle.'

The Emperor was very much agitated by this news; when he had collected himself, he asked how the army had been received. 'Amid cheers for the Alliance, your Majesty. The Confederate troops in a body have joined our flag, and the people came in crowds from all sides to bring provisions to the army, for which we paid in ready money.'

I could easily read in the Emperor's features the conflicting feelings which this news excited. After a longer pause, he took my hand and said:—'Success crowns the undertaking: it remains for success to justify what you have done. As one of the Allied monarchs I have nothing more to say to you; but as a man I declare to you that you have grieved me in a way that you can never repair.'

I remained quiet, and replied to his Majesty that my conscience did not reproach me, because his glory was as dear to me as the great cause which was his as well as that of all Europe.

'You do not know how you have grieved me,' said the Emperor hastily. 'You do not know the peculiar circumstances of my position.'

'I know them,' I replied, 'and I believe I know

them fully. It is not for you to reproach me, your
Majesty. The regret is much more on my side. Why
did your Majesty not let me know what I ought to have
known, even if it were only to oppose it? Your Majesty
would have been spared many griefs, and your friend
the Emperor also.'

'The thing is done,' said the Emperor quietly; 'it
is good from a military point of view, so then let personal considerations yield to the common good. Let us
go straight on to the end in view, and talk no more
about it.'

And, in fact, we did not talk any more about it, and
the Emperor Alexander never mentioned the subject to
the Emperor Francis.

The military arrangements for carrying out the
operations were quickly made. The Emperor of Russia
asked as a favour that his guard, which formed the head
of the Russian columns, might pass the bridge of Basle
on the Greek New Year's Day (January 13, 1814).
His wish was granted, although the general operation
suffered some useless delay in consequence.

Our stay in Basle had nothing remarkable in it but
the arrival of Lord Castlereagh. It was here that a
few hours' conversation sufficed to lay the foundation of
a good feeling between this upright and enlightened
statesman and myself, which the following eventful
years cemented and enlarged.

I found Lord Castlereagh not quite thoroughly informed of the real state of affairs on the Continent.
His straightforward feeling, free from all prejudice and
prepossession, and his justice and benevolence gave him
a quick insight into the truth of things. I soon saw
that his ideas about the reconstruction of France in a
manner compatible with the general interests of Europe

did not materially differ from mine. Thus the residence in Basle was merely a preparation for the political scene which was soon inaugurated in Langres.

Residence in Langres.

Langres, the crowning point of the Vosges where they overlook the plains of France, and the heights of the Ardennes, were fixed on by the Frankfort decrees as the strategic line where the third operation was to begin. We entered Langres on January 25, 1814, and the following days were occupied with negotiations of the greatest importance. These would remain unknown to the world for ever if I did not record them here.

As the monarchs and their cabinets were here together, no protocols were drawn up, so that no written trace exists of proceedings which had the most important consequences. The correspondence of Lord Castlereagh with his cabinet may contain some fragments, but it cannot give the complete course, for the principal questions were only discussed between the Emperor of Russia and myself

Soon after the arrival of the monarchs in Langres, I was informed by the sagacious and far-seeing men of the cabinet of the Emperor Alexander that this monarch was much agitated at the necessity of coming to a conclusion with respect to the future form of government to be established in France, which indeed was the most important of all questions. The overthrow of Napoleon seemed to be inevitable. The attempt to come to a treaty of peace which should maintain him on the throne had been unsuccessful from his own fault, and would in no way have attained the objects of the great Alliance—the object, namely, of establishing a state of peace based on the due consideration of the relations of the Powers to each other, and promising as much durability as can be expected from any political creation.

Every peace with Napoleon which would have thrown him back to the old boundaries of France, and which would have deprived him of districts that had been conquered before he came to power, would only have been a ridiculous armistice, and would at once have been repelled by him. There remained, therefore, only three possibilities: the recall of the Bourbons; a regency till the majority of Napoleon's son; the nomination of a third person to the throne of France.

Everything—just rights as well as reason, the interest of France as well as the general interest of Europe— spoke in favour of the first course. The Emperor of Austria did not for a moment doubt this. The same thing cannot be said of his Majesty the Emperor of Russia. The revolutionary spirits who surrounded this monarch, and who at that time exercised a pernicious and only too decisive influence on the tendencies of his mind, had laboured for a long time in a direction opposed to the legitimate claims of the Bourbon family. They ceased not to represent its return as a vain undertaking. The Emperor was convinced of this. Difficulties easy to be conceived were raised against the accession to the throne of Napoleon's son, then a little child. The man who was at once suggested for the third of the supposed cases was the Crown Prince of Sweden. The intrigues of himself and of his friends had not been without their effects. His previous life and career rendered him accessible to the revolutionary party; and there is no doubt that Laharpe himself would have raised him to the throne had not his thoroughly republican feeling and sentiment preferred a return to that constitution which best corresponded with his mode of thinking.

I allowed the first days to pass ; they were devoted to purely military arrangements. The exaggerated zeal of the Prussian generals needed to be restrained. We at last settled on the plan which promised most success against the resistance to be expected from Napoleon's genius when driven to its last defences. It was resolved that the Austrian army and the greater part of the Russian and Prussian Guards should form one great army. Another was formed by the Prussian army, reinforced by two Russian corps. The object of all the operations was to be—Paris. The line of operation of Prince Schwarzenberg was to be in the direction of the Seine—that of General Blücher the direction of the Marne. If Napoleon offered battle to one or other of the armies, the one attacked was not to accept the challenge, but to wait till the Allies came to its help. The corps under the command of General Bubna, should take Lyons, and keep in check and beat the army opposed to him under Augereau.

When these dispositions were determined on, I was sent for, one evening, by the Emperor of Russia. He began the conversation with the explanation of the chief reasons which had prevented him from sooner expressing his thoughts to the Allies regarding the future government of France. He imparted to me his particular wish, for these same reasons, to learn on the very spot itself the true feeling of the French nation. 'It is against the Bourbons,' said the Emperor to me ; ' and to bring these back to a throne which they had not known how to keep would be to expose France, and eventually all Europe, to another Revolution, of which no one can foretell the consequences. To choose a new

ruler is a very difficult undertaking for a foreigner. My
resolution, therefore, is taken. The operations against
Paris must be continued with vigour; we must take
possession of the city. On the approach of this event,
which will crown the military successes of the Alliance,
it will be necessary to issue a Proclamation to the
French people, declaring our determination to have
nothing to do with the choice of a form of government,
or the selection of a ruler. At the same time we must
summon the original assemblies, and demand that a
proper number of deputies should be sent to Paris to
decide both these points in the name of the nation.'

I did not think it prudent directly to oppose a scheme
which apparently was not merely the Emperor's own
idea. As it was most important to me to learn the
details of this plan, I only expressed my doubt whether
its results would ever answer the expectations of his
Majesty. 'Bonaparte,' I observed to the Emperor, ' has
mastered the Revolution ; the plan of calling the nation
to deliberate on questions concerning the foundation
of the social edifice of France, and thereby causing,
as it were, a second Convention, would unchain the
Revolution again, and that can never be the object of
the Alliance, nor the meaning of their deliberations.'

The Emperor replied, with vivacity, that my observations would be correct if the monarchs did not hold
in their hands the measures by which revolutionary
evils could be restrained. ' We are in France,' he continued, ' and our armies are numerous : they will inti-
midate the agitators. The deputies of the nation will
only have to give their opinion on two questions—namely,
the form of government and the selection of a ruler.
The Republic is at an end. It has fallen by its own
excesses. The Prince whom the nation will give to itself

will have less difficulty in establishing his authority. The authority of Napoleon is broken, and no one will have anything more to do with it. A more essential point will be to direct the assembly aright. I have in readiness, the man most suitable for this, most fitted for an affair, which would perhaps be impossible to a novice. We entrust the direction of this matter to Laharpe.'

I thought this the right moment to attack the question.

'This plan,' I replied, 'will never be accepted by the Emperor, my master; and if he should give way, I should immediately lay my resignation at his feet. The carrying out of this plan would cause France and the whole of Europe years of confusion and sorrow. If M. Laharpe thinks himself able to answer for the result, he is mistaken; and I speak only of the material disadvantages, for what will become of Europe even from the mere starting of the principle on which the idea rests? The confidence which your Majesty has just shown me by giving me an insight into your views on the most important question of the day,' I continued, ' demands from me the most perfect candour. What I am now going to say to you, your Majesty, is what the Emperor Francis thinks. Napoleon's power is broken, and will not rise again. This is the fate of the power of a usurper when a crisis arrives. When the overthrow of the Empire comes, there will be only the Bourbons to take possession again of their undying rights. They will do it by.the power of events and the wish of the nation; about which, in my opinion, there can be no doubt. The Emperor Francis will never favour any other dynasty.'

The Emperor Alexander dismissed me with the charge to report our conversation to my master. It was

midnight.   On my return, I found at my house, Count
Nesselrode and General Pozzo di Borgo.   They knew
that I had spent the evening with the Emperor Alexander.   I trusted them sufficiently to inform them of the
subject of our conversation.   They were both much
agitated, and begged me never to relax my opposition
to ideas which they judged as I did, both from a consideration of their real meaning and the source from
which alone they could have sprung.

I was authorised by the Emperor Francis to go so
far as to threaten the immediate withdrawal of his
army.

The following evening, I went again to the Emperor
of Russia.   I had heard during the day that he was much
excited, but did not speak to any of his ministers on the
subject of our conversation of the preceding day.   His
Majesty enquired from me what were the views of the
Emperor of Austria on this subject.

'To answer your Majesty in a few words,' I replied,
'I can only repeat what I said yesterday.   The Emperor
is against any appeal to the nation—to a people who
would be in the false position of deliberating in face of
seven hundred thousand foreign bayonets.   The Emperor does not see either, what could be the subject of
deliberation—the legitimate King is there.'

The Emperor Alexander composed himself, and said,
'I do not insist on my idea against the wish of my
allies : I have spoken according to my conscience ; time
will do the rest ; it will also teach us who was right.'

Seeing the Emperor in such a favourable mood, I
gave my thoughts full course, and showed him the
dangers which would have been inseparable from a plan
which would have left no choice between breaking up
the Alliance just when its efforts were about to be

crowned with success, and undermining the foundations of social order and throwing Europe into confusions worse than those which attended the first outbreak of the Revolution. The Emperor followed my argument step by step, and combated what was most opposed to his ideas; but we parted good friends.

I should not have described this circumstance so fully, if ignorant persons from party spirit had not, in the important question of the internal arrangement of France, attributed to the Emperor Francis and his cabinet views and intentions which had no foundation whatever, thus placing the attitude of Austria and her allies in a light quite opposed to truth. The feeling which guided Austria was well considered, and was free from ambitious or sanguinary feelings, and entirely devoted to the great task of attaining and securing a state of peace for the European continent resting on solid grounds. This was the direction in which the cabinet thought and acted in its political course, as well as in the operations of the war.

The rest of our stay in Langres was devoted to arranging the military operations. It was beyond doubt that, at any rate at first, Napoleon would limit his defence to the approaches to Paris, and that therefore the campaign would open on the Aube.

The news which came to us from those parts of the country behind the Allied armies, as well as from other parts of France, as to the feelings of the nation, were confirmed by the observations which we ourselves were able to make concerning this important question, at the place where the head-quarters were stationed. The prevailing feeling of the people consisted in the wish for an early conclusion of the operations, and by far the larger majority was for the return of the Bourbons.

The political question was discussed no more by the Emperor of Russia and his allies. The course of events shows how useful it would have been if a regular plan for our future attitude had been made at the right time, resting on the principle of a restoration of the legitimate power. The advantage, however, of having removed for the moment so fatal an idea was too great not to be very satisfactory. The attempt to go farther would have miscarried, and would have endangered the necessary harmony between the Powers, which in the very midst of France itself were occupied in an undertaking still liable to all the chances of war.

There was no danger that the nation might wish the maintenance of the Imperial government. Our care was limited to a successful termination of the war, and the final result of the great undertaking we committed to a Power higher than that of men.

Congress of Chatillon.

Few negotiations of the year 1814 were better known to the public than those of Chatillon. The acts of the Congress have been given to the public, and discussed by the historians of all parties. The following is the truth with regard to the spirit which guided the cabinets in this juncture.

The four Allied Powers, harmonious as their proceedings appeared, were nevertheless divided in their secret views about many points of high and decided importance.

The Emperor of Austria had directed his thoughts and wishes only to a state of things which enabled him to hope that the political peace of Europe would be secured by a return to the balance of power and political equilibrium which had been entirely destroyed by the French conquests during the Revolution and the Empire.   At the time we are speaking of—namely, after the concentration of the operations between the Seine and Marne—the overthrow of the French Empire was beyond doubt for every politician who did not give himself up to illusions.   The return of the Bourbons and the reduction of France to her old boundaries seemed to the Emperor Francis and his cabinet the only tenable propositions, since they alone would gua- rantee a peace founded on legitimacy.   Austria was, on this fundamental point, in perfect harmony with the British Government.

The ideas of the Emperor Alexander, as we have seen, hovered sometimes in the mists of a vague liberal- ism, and at other times were the result of personal or accidental influences.

Prussia was filled with thoughts of conquest and with a thirst for the revenge of all her sorrows of the last few years, which was perhaps natural.   The King and Prince Hardenberg agreed much better with our views and those of the English as to the dynasty to be placed on the French throne, than with the exaggerated ideas of the Emperor of Russia.

Napoleon now felt that it was quite necessary to make use of the last chances of obtaining a peaceful adjustment.

My own feeling in pressing the opening of formal negotiations was only the continuation of that which had directed my calculations and my political attitude since the beginning of the year 1813.   I had so thorough a knowledge of the inclination of the mass of the French people, of the feeling of the Army, and also of the direction of Napoleon's mind, that I saw only great advantages from these attempts at negotiation, without any fear that an untimely settlement would delay the return to a better order of things.

I therefore used my influence to carry out the declarations which had been made by the Powers in Frankfort since the beginning of the year. In this matter I was greatly assisted by the perfect agreement of Lord Castlereagh's views with my own.

I brought about the appointment of Count Stadion as Plenipotentiary of Austria. The other cabinets followed this example, and their leaders remained in the head-quarters of the monarchs; with the exception only of Lord Castlereagh, who could not give up to another so important a matter as the representation of Great Britain at the Congress where the foundations of a general peace were to be arranged.

It soon appeared that Napoleon, notwithstanding the enormous difficulties of his position, did not seriously think of peace.

He gave a proof of how easily his hopes revived again, by the extraordinary importance which he attributed to the trifling success of the skirmish of Montereau. The day after this fight, he wrote a letter to the Emperor of Austria quite in the tone as if written after one of his former great victories. Among other things, he was weak enough to give in this letter a calculation of the losses of the Allies on the day of the battle of Montereau which, in vain-glorious boasting, far surpassed the fabulous accounts of his 'war-bulletins.'

The course of military events put an end to the conferences at Chatillon.

The Council of War at Bar-sur-l'Aube.

The great Austrian army had, in consequence of the battle of Montereau, become separated from Blücher's army. Obliged to evacuate Troyes and to retreat to Bar-sur-l'Aube, the three monarchs held a conference at which, besides their Majesties and their ministers, several generals of the Allied armies assisted. The military measures to be taken were there discussed with great animation.

The King of Prussia insisted most energetically that the three armies should unite and make an immediate attack upon Paris. The Emperor Francis, Prince Schwarzenberg, and I defended the opposite proposal. The plan which we had hitherto followed so successfully seemed too good to be hastily renounced. Its object was to avoid risking the fate of the campaign on the chance of one general battle, but gradually to exhaust Napoleon's strength. This plan, though slow in its operation, seemed certain of success. Events have proved this to be the case. A subordinate motive contributed to the urgency of the Prussian party. The army of Marshal Blücher was already on the road to Paris—all their desire was to be the first to occupy Paris. This army and its leaders were so exasperated that even the latter did not shrink from the idea of abandoning Paris to the fury of the soldiers, whom it would have been impossible to restrain in the first moment of their success. Such a consideration could not be left out of our reckoning, and if prudence had not restrained us from venturing the fate of the campaign on one great battle, as Napoleon so much desired, the intentions of the Prussians with regard to Paris, which were no secret from anyone, would alone have been sufficient to prevent us from yielding.

The discussion was animated, and was led by the King of Prussia with some heat. The Emperor Alexander hesitated to favour either one side or the other. Only in consequence of an energetic declaration of the Emperor Francis, which I supported with perfect openness, and with all my might, did the Russian monarch agree to Austria's views. He offered to take the office of secretary, and I dictated to him the points agreed upon as follows :

1. No battle is to be fought near Bar-sur-l'Aube.

2. Blücher shall continue his separate movement.

3. The great army shall continue its march by Chaumont and Langres.

4. The continuation of this movement will depend on circumstances.

5. To inform Blücher of the movements decided on for the great army, and that Wintzingerode and Bülow are to be at his command.

6. To give the necessary orders to Wintzingerode and Bülow.

7. To give to Blücher a certain latitude in his movements, provided always that military prudence be observed.

The council of war separated, but the Prussian party were very much out of humour.

As I have no intention of entering into the details of military operations, I shall here limit myself to those circumstances which have a political bearing. The battle which Prince Schwarzenberg accepted near Arcis proved to be a mere skirmish with the outposts, for Napoleon broke it off as soon as he had convinced himself that both the Austrian and Prussian armies would take part in the fight. To his astonishment the commander-in-chief saw, from the heights behind Arcis, the French army in full retreat, eastwards.

The Emperor of Austria remained behind in Bar-sur-l'Aube with the intention of leaving it for Arcis, if a battle should take place. His Majesty had all the ministers with him, except Count Nesselrode.

In the meantime arrived an adjutant, Count Paar, sent to head-quarters by Prince Schwarzenberg. He brought the new arrangements for the generals in command. Prince Schwarzenberg, having crossed the Aube, and made certain that Napoleon was continuing his march eastwards, proposed to the Emperor of Russia and the King of Prussia to attack Paris with the united forces of the Allies. But by this movement the Austrian army and part of the Russian were in danger of being cut off from their line of operations. Napoleon might have two plans. He might either attack the rearguard of the army near Nancy, or the fortified places to the east, and, reinforced by their occupation, he might begin a new war at some place between the Rhine and the invading army.

The Field-Marshal informed the Emperor that if this operation was successful, he would take the city of Paris, and remain there—if unsuccessful, he would retire upon Belgium. He begged his Majesty at the same time to make the necessary arrangements, and to inform the military commissariat of the dangers which threatened them. Count Paar brought the order to the chief officer of the Russian commissariat, who had remained in Bar-sur-l'Aube, to repair immediately to the Russian head-quarters. The first thought of the Emperor was to go himself to head-quarters without loss of time; but by a simple calculation it was soon

seen that this was not feasible. At the time of Count
Paar's arrival the army was already a day's march on
the way to Paris, and therefore the Emperor could only
have reached the head-quarters at the third halting-
place, while the country between was open to French
stragglers. His Majesty was obliged, with great regret,
to await the course of events. I considered for a long
time whether I should run the risk of attempting to
reach the head-quarters myself. The impossibility of
securing the necessary change of horses for making a
three days' march without delay, prevented me from
carrying out my wishes. Count Paar had taken the
precaution of securing beforehand the change of horses
required for his own journey. He arrived safely at
head-quarters, and carried with him the full consent of
the Emperor to the Field-Marshal's plan.

The chief of the Russian commissariat was seized
the day after his departure by some French cavalry,
who had attacked the rear of the great Allied army. In
the course of the same night we received, at 2 o'clock
A.M., the news that Napoleon had gone eastwards as far
as St.-Dizier, and that on receipt of the news of the
bold movement against Paris he had turned into the
road to Bar-sur-l'Aube. This movement showed that
Napoleon's eccentric march had no other object but to
cause the commander of the Austrian army to retreat,
by threatening his connecting line of operations.
Napoleon was mistaken; and when he heard of the
march of the army to Paris, he exclaimed, ' A fine
move! I should not have expected it from a general
of the Coalition.'

Preparations were immediately made for departure
from Bar-sur-l'Aube, and at 4 o'clock in the morning the
Emperor and his ministers set out for Dijon, with the

small escort of a few battalions who were on their
march to join the great army, and one of which had
happened to arrive in Bar the night before. This
march brought us nearer to the army of the hereditary
Prince of Hesse-Homburg, some troops of which were
now in Dijon.

Stay in Dijon.

As the Emperor did not wish to be long on the road,
he posted from Chatillon to Dijon. We made the last
part of the way in two post-chaises, among a population who were greatly astonished at the arrival of his
Imperial Majesty, and at the confidence which allowed
us to come among them without escort. The impression made by this unexpected arrival of the Emperor in
Dijon was the same as it had been on the road. We
arrived at 4 o'clock in the morning in Dijon, and the
Emperor alighted at the palace of the Prefecture. We
were obliged to mention the Emperor's name to gain
admittance. In a few hours the populace rushed into
the open space before the Prefecture, and a great
Royalist agitation took place. His Majesty called upon
the different parties to keep quiet, and forbade every
kind of reaction. These orders were strictly followed.

Some days after our arrival in the town, Baron
Wessenberg arrived, who had fallen into the hands of
General Piré, on his return from an embassy to England.

The country to the west of Dijon was unsafe;
General Allix commanded there a corps of mobilised
National Guards. Some troops collected from different
directions and, united with those who had left Bar with
us, sufficed to guard our stay in Dijon, where we
remained till we received the news of the capitulation
of Paris. Nearly at the same time with this news the

Duke of Cadore (Champagny) was announced to deliver a communication from Napoleon to the Emperor. I did not see him, because his Majesty had ordered me to start for Paris without delay. This mission had no success.

The news of the capitulation of Paris caused a great sensation in Dijon. The courtyard of the hotel where I lived was soon filled with thousands of men. A deputation came to ask me whether it was permitted to set up the royal colours. His Majesty gave his consent, and I communicated it to the assembled public. Shortly afterwards the royal flag waved in Dijon. I departed in company with Lord Castlereagh and Chancellor Hardenberg.

Arrival in Paris.

I arrived in Paris on April 10. A few minutes afterwards I went to the Emperor Alexander. He had taken up his abode in the hotel of Prince Talleyrand. His Majesty informed me of his communications with Napoleon since the entrance of the Allied armies into Paris, and of the presence of the Marshals Ney and Macdonald, Napoleon's plenipotentiaries, in Paris, for the conclusion of a treaty with the Allies, in which he renounced the throne of France, and accepted the sovereignty of the island of Elba.

I expressed my astonishment at the last point of this agreement. I represented to him how many unpleasantnesses would arise from an arrangement by which a residence was chosen for the dethroned Emperor so near to the country he had formerly governed. It was easy to support my apprehensions by considerations arising from Napoleon's character, and others which were made evident by the force of circumstances.

The Emperor of Russia met my argument with reasons which did him great credit, but were little suited to tranquillise me as to my predictions. One of his arguments was that without insult the word of a soldier and a sovereign could not be doubted. I declared to his Majesty that I did not feel authorised to take upon myself a decision of such great consequence for the future repose of France and of Europe without having received the commands of the Emperor, my master. 'This cannot now be done,' replied the Emperor Alexander warmly. 'In the expectation of your arrival, and of Lord Castlereagh's, I have put off the signature of the treaty for several days; this must be brought to a conclusion in the course of the evening; the marshals must deliver the act to Napoleon this very night. If the signing of this act is not completed, hostilities will begin again to-morrow, and God knows what the result may be. Napoleon is at the head of his army at Fontainebleau, and it is not unknown to him that the act is approved by myself and the King of Prussia; I cannot take back my word. On the other hand, I cannot force you to sign the document which has been already drawn up, and which Nesselrode will lay before you; but you will incur a very heavy responsibility if you do not sign.' I told his Majesty that before I resolved what was to be done, I wished to consult with Prince Schwarzenberg and Lord Castlereagh.

After this consultation, I returned to the Emperor Alexander. I said to him, 'The negotiation between your Majesty, the King of Prussia, and Napoleon has gone too far for my opposition to stop it. Prince Schwarzenberg has taken part in the preliminary discussions; the conference in which this treaty is to be

signed has actually met.   I will go to it, and there place
my name to a treaty which in less than two years will
bring us back again to the battle-field.'

Events proved that I had made a mistake of only a
year.   The treaty was signed in the course of that
evening.

The terms of this treaty have been very variously
judged, and it could not be otherwise.   The truth is,
that a display of magnanimity was in this case out of
place, and the facility with which the Emperor Alexander surrendered himself to the force of illusions had
the same effect on his side as the pressure of circumstances had in compelling the Emperor Napoleon to
sign it.   I shall always consider the conference between
the Plenipotentiaries which preceded the signing of the
convention as the most remarkable scene of my public
life.   The articles were determined on, except in some
unimportant deviations in the composition, at the very
opening of the sitting.   I did not conceal from my colleagues the impression which the investing of Napoleon
with the island of Elba made upon me.   There was
not one of them who did not share it, and the language of Napoleon's two plenipotentiaries differed little
from our own.   The feelings which they expressed on
this subject were perfectly correct and free from all illusions.   On my return from the conference, I despatched
a courier to the Emperor Francis, who at once left
Dijon and set out for Paris, where the hotel of the Princess Borghese had been prepared for his reception.

Commissioners of the Allies accompanied Napoleon
to his new destination.   The Imperial General von
Koller, who acted in this capacity in the name of
Austria, on one occasion, by his presence of mind and
courage, saved Napoleon from dangers which threatened

his life in the midst of the hot-blooded country-people of Provence.

The monarchs placed the Empress Marie Louise and the King of Rome under the protection of her father. Marie Louise went to Schönbrunn.

Entrance of Louis XVIII. into Paris, and the condition of France after the return of the Bourbons.

On May 4 King Louis XVIII. made his entrance into Paris. I had placed myself, with Prince Schwarzenberg, at a window in the Rue Montmartre to see the procession go by. It made a most painful impression upon me. A contrast prevailed between the gloomy countenances of the Imperial Guard who preceded and followed the royal carriage, and that of the King beaming with studied affability, which seemed to reflect the general feeling of the country. The attitude of the crowd in the streets completed the picture in this respect. The most opposite feelings were depicted in their faces, and found their expression in the cry ' *Vive le Roi* ' from the side of the Royalists, and the sullen silence of the enemies of the monarchy. I could almost have thought that the King was too eager to respond with his movement of salutation to so mixed a manifestation of feeling.

The three monarchs went immediately to pay their visits to the King, and immediately afterwards I presented myself at the Tuileries. The King received me in his closet. In the course of conversation I could not help remarking to him that in this same room, sitting at the same writing table, surrounded by the same articles of furniture, I had passed many hours with Napoleon. ' Your Majesty,' I said to the King, ' seems, however, to be quite at home here.'

'It must be allowed,' answered the King, 'that Napoleon was a very good tenant; he made everything most comfortable; he has arranged everything excellently for me.'

I spent two hours with his Majesty, and left the King without having at all the satisfactory impression which I ought to have had with regard to the future of France. We talked over the maps which had just been published, of the difficulties which, according to my views, had to be faced in carrying them out, of the mood of the public, &c. I therefore had the opportunity of convincing myself that the King had decided views on all those subjects which differed from my own in more than one point of importance.

Time has, more indeed than I could have desired, verified the views which I even then held to be correct.

The question whether the return of the Bourbon family to France was according to the wish of the country has received very different replies. I do not hesitate to affirm that it was accepted most willingly by the enormous majority of the people, and the cause of this feeling lay so deep in the nature of the case that it could not be otherwise.*

France has gone through the phases of social Revolution in a comparatively very short time. These phases, between the years 1789 and 1814, may be

---

* During my stay in Paris in 1825, when I was summoned thither by a domestic affliction, I was received by King Charles X. After dinner we spoke much of the past, and lively recollections, called forth by the very rooms in which we stood, rushed into my mind. 'I remember,' I remarked among other things to the King, 'that in 1810 in this very *salon* I was sitting with Napoleon, and that, when we came to speak of the Bourbons, Napoleon said to me: "Do you know why Louis XVIII. is not sitting opposite to you? It is only because it is I who am sitting here. No other person could maintain his position; and if ever I disappear in consequence of a catastrophe, no one but a Bourbon could sit here."'

divided into three epochs : the first, from 1789 to 1792, was the epoch of the overthrow of centuries of ancient institutions and the creation of a Republic modelled after the illusive ideas of the eighteenth century ; the second, from 1792 to 1804, was the attempt at a Republican government ; and lastly, the Empire, between the years 1804 and 1814, has fulfilled the end which Napoleon's vast genius proposed to itself, and the kingdom of France is once more established on a monarchical foundation.

With the exception of a handful of incorrigible enthusiasts, the republican form of government had few supporters in the country; they had disappeared, first in consequence of the Reign of Terror, which had raised itself on the ruins of the throne, the old institutions and everything which had outlasted the governments of Louis XIII. and XIV., and the moral decay and the governmental disorders of the Regency and the time of Louis XV., and then the depravity and weakness of the Directorate. The form of government which Napoleon had introduced was agreeable to all France, but it was weary of wars of which it could see no end. The return of the Bourbons was not longed for in the sense which the Royalists attributed to this feeling, and the Royalist party itself had much diminished during the course of five-and-twenty years. It was longed for by the friends of public order and political peace— that is, by the great majority of the nation, which in all times and in all countries ever places first in their calculations the true interests of the Fatherland.

Therefore the real difficulties of the monarchy on the reappearance of the government did not lie in the public feeling, but in the line of conduct which it had taken. The return to what was called ' the old *Régime* ' was impossible, because nothing was left of it but the remembrance of the causes of its decay. Neither had the Bourbons ever thought of it, and even the name was at no time anything more than a brand wherewith to terrify the masses.*

* Here ends the manuscript 'On the History of the Alliances.' The following chapter is taken from the text of the 'Guide.'—ED.

The Allies enter Paris in triumph in April 1814.

Metternich's office.

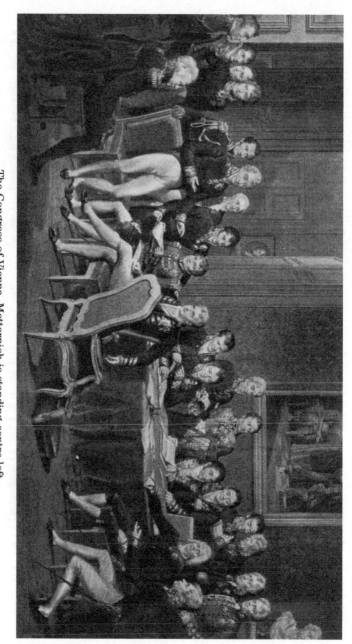

The Congress of Vienna. Metternich is standing centre left.

CHAPTER IX.

THE DAWN OF PEACE.

I SHOULD exceed the limits I have proposed to myself in the present work, if I were to enter into the details of the negotiations which preceded the Peace of May 30, 1814.

The Peace itself bore the stamp of the moderation of the monarchs and their cabinets—a moderation which did not arise from weakness, but from the resolve to secure a lasting peace to Europe. The situation was one of those when, for the attainment of an object, it is more dangerous to do too much than too little.

Only a calculation resting on firm foundations can secure the success of an undertaking. It had been proved that the peace to be concluded with France could only be looked at either as a revenge on the country, or as establishing the greatest possible political equilibrium between the Powers. That the Emperor Francis prepared, in perfect harmony with my conviction, to bring about the solution of the problem in the latter direction, had been proved by the conditions under which Austria entered the Alliance. The rejection of the system of conquest, and the establishment of the system of restitution and equivalents in the forming of kingdoms and states, remove all doubt on this point.

I was beforehand well aware that the Imperial cabinet would, from this manner of looking at the whole question, come into conflict with all kinds of political swindlers and with the separate interests of single governments, but I did not allow my course to be altered thereby. Just as the entrance of Austria into the Quadruple Alliance had formed the foundation for the Peace of Paris, that peace formed the foundation for the settlement of the difficult problem by the Vienna Congress.

After the signature of the Paris Peace, I went with the Emperor Alexander and the King of Prussia to England, taking with me the excuses of the Emperor Francis to the Prince Regent. I also received myself a personal invitation from the Prince Regent. Twenty years had elapsed since I had first visited that country, and made the acquaintance of the then Prince of Wales. I wished to see England again, to behold with my own eyes the impression which the changes in the political situation on the Continent must have made there, and at the same time to confer with the English Cabinet on the negotiations preliminary to the Congress of Vienna.

After an absence of several months, I arrived again in Vienna on July 18. The moral impression made on me by the mood in which I found the country was not elevating, but so far satisfactory that it convinced me that the political line which I followed was right, in reference to the position of our own empire as well as to the securing of a long general peace. Austria was endur-ing the after-pains of a two-and-twenty years' war, and felt her very existence in danger. The people of Austria, always calm and reasonable, had imagined that the union of the Emperor's daughter with Napoleon would have been a pledge of peace, and they yielded reluctantly to the fate of a new war. The result to be expected from this war seemed to the populace to be nothing more than a second edition of the former peace in rather a different form.

What a striking contrast was there in the situation of Prussia as compared with that of Austria! Only a dreamer could put them on the same level, and to the dreamers I have never belonged. The domain which opened the widest field for men of this class at the beginning of the Congress was Germany, and with this conviction I looked continually in that direction during the weeks preceding the opening of the Congress.

I have already mentioned the saying of the Emperor that a German political body must be called into existence in the form of a Confederation, and have asserted that this had practically the value of a *conditio sine quâ non* as to the first entrance of Austria into the Alliance. The direction I had to follow was therefore clearly pointed out. The only question was, the choice of means for the attainment of the end. This matter was made extremely difficult by the Powers which opposed it. In the first rank stood the separatist efforts of Prussia; then the dread of the German princes of any limitation of their sovereign rights; and, lastly, the aspirations which had emerged in North Germany and the Rhine Provinces since 1806—aspirations which showed themselves partly in decided democratic tendencies, and partly can only be described as ' *deutsch-thümelnde Gelüste* ' (predilections for German nationality and principles). In the conflict which arose, the aristocratic tendencies blended with the democratic in the mind of Freiherr von Stein played a peculiar and prominent part. Among all these parties the latter, however, was the most divided, both with regard to end and means. To the dictates of party I paid no other attention than to be conscious of their existence, and to redouble our efforts to keep our own path clear.

I summoned the few officials of the time of the Empire to a consultation upon German questions, but I was soon convinced that I could find in them the aid only of mere antiquarianism. I determined, therefore, to take my stand immovably upon the general principles of the Confederation, and to relegate its more special provisions to the German deputies at the Congress.

This Congress was opened on November 3, 1814, by a simple unpretending conference not at all corresponding to the expectations of a public greedy for ' spectacle.' *

The Plenipotentiaries of the different states and countries begged me to undertake the direction of the negotiations. I undertook that office in the conviction that the questions to be submitted to the Congress could only be settled if brought forward in systematic order, everything unnecessary being rigorously rejected, with a clear apprehension of everything that time and circumstances demanded. I submitted a scheme for the order of proceeding, which embraced—

(a) The consultations of the members of the Quadruple Alliance and of France, under the designation of the ' *Comité des cinq Puissances.*'

---

* The public had taken it into its head that the meetings of the Plenipotentiaries at the Congress would be held in the great Ball-room of the Imperial Palace, and that the public would be admitted to the galleries which run round it.

(*b*) The meetings of the Plenipotentiaries of these five Powers with the Plenipotentiaries of Spain, Portugal, and Sweden, under the designation of the ' *Assemblée des huit Cours*,' and their connection with the representatives of the other states.

(*c*) The institution of a commission to be formed from the Plenipotentiaries of the German states, specially devoted to the regulation of German affairs.

This form was accepted; and under its protection the grave matters submitted to the assembly were brought to a solution.

The history of the Congress is written in its Acts and in its results, and has no place in these pages. It has experienced the destiny of all remarkable events, it has not escaped the criticism of the prejudiced, or the censure of the superficial; and, in order to estimate the importance of its transactions, the consideration may suffice that from this Congress the foundations of the political peace which has subsisted for eight-and-thirty years have proceeded, and that its most important decrees have been able not only to defy the storms which arose in the intermediate period, but even to survive the revolutions of the year 1848.*

The news received on March 7, 1815, that Napoleon had left the island of Elba contributed much to the acceleration of the negotiations just begun in the Congress, and especially to a more speedy agreement of the German courts with regard to the Acts of Confedera-

---

* The *mot* of Field-Marshal the Prince de Ligne, ' *le Congrès danse mais ne marche pas*,' has gone the round of the newspapers. During the Congress a number of crowned heads with numerous retinues and a crowd of tourists assembled within the walls of Vienna. To provide social recreation for them was one of the duties of the Imperial Court; that these festivities had no connection with the labours of the Congress, and did not interfere with them, is proved by the short duration of the Congress, which accomplished its work in five months.

tion. The course of the affair was as follows, and the decision for war was taken in almost as short a time as I shall require for describing it.

I received the first news of Napoleon having left Elba in the following manner. A conference between the Plenipotentiaries of the five Powers took place in my house on the night of March 6, and lasted till three o'clock in the morning. Since the Cabinets had met in Vienna, I had given my servant orders that if a courier arrived at night he was not to awake me. In spite of this order, the servant brought me at six o'clock in the morning a despatch, sent by courier, and marked *urgent*. When I saw on the envelope the words ' from the Consul-general at Genoa,' having been only two hours in bed, I laid the despatch unopened on the nearest table, and turned round again to sleep. Once disturbed, however, sleep would not come again. About half-past seven I resolved to open the despatch. It contained the information in six lines: ' The English Commissary, Campbell, has just appeared in the harbour, to inquire whether Napoleon has been seen in Genoa, as he has disappeared from the island of Elba; this question being answered in the negative, the English ship has again put out to sea.'

I was dressed in a few minutes, and before eight o'clock I was with the Emperor. He read the despatch, and said to me quietly and calmly, as he always did on great occasions: ' Napoleon seems to wish to play the adventurer: that is his concern; ours is to secure to the world that peace which he has disturbed for years. Go without delay to the Emperor of Russia and the King of Prussia, and tell them that I am ready to order my army to march back to France. I do not doubt but that both monarchs will agree with me.'

At a quarter-past eight I was with the Emperor
Alexander, who dismissed me with the same words as
the Emperor Francis had used. At half-past eight I
received a similar declaration from the mouth of King
Frederic William III. At nine o'clock I was at my
house again, where I had directed Field-Marshal Prince
Schwarzenberg to meet me. At ten o'clock the ministers of the four Powers came at my request. At the
same hour adjutants were already on their way, in all
directions, to order the armies to halt who were returning home.

Thus war was decided on in less than an hour.
When the ministers assembled at my house, the event
was unknown to them. Talleyrand was the first to
enter. I gave him the despatch from Genoa to read.
He remained calm, and the following laconic conversation took place between us:

Talleyrand.—' Do you know where Napoleon is
going?'

Metternich.—' The despatch does not say anything
about it.'

Talleyrand.—' He will embark somewhere on the
coast of Italy, and throw himself into Switzerland.'

Metternich.—' He will go straight to Paris.'

This is the history in its full simplicity.

One great stumbling-block in the arrangement of
the German territorial questions at the Vienna Congress
proved to be the agreement made at Kalisch between
the Emperor of Russia and the King of Prussia with
regard to the incorporation of the kingdom of Saxony
with the Prussian monarchy. When at last the Powers
had come to an agreement between themselves about this
important question, the consent of the King of Saxony
not having been yet received, the news arrived in Vienna

of Napoleon's escape. The Congress commissioned the
Duke of Wellington, Prince Talleyrand, and myself to
gain the consent of King Frederick Augustus, who was
at that time in Presburg. We repaired to the much-
harassed Prince, and concluded the business in a few
hours.

As a circumstance very characteristic of the time,
I will mention that the Duke of Wellington, on the day
of our return to Vienna, was present at a review at Presburg of a regiment of cuirassiers, which was going to
the Rhine, whose march through Vienna on their way
to Hungary the Duke had also seen.

In looking back, quite impartially, on the results of
the Congress now concluded, I may be allowed to say
a few words.

The peculiar characteristic of the French Revolution, from its very beginning, was that it was thoroughly
social. Its political character, of which Napoleon was
the highest expression, was at first foreign to it. Napoleon in endeavouring to restore France to internal order,
knew no bounds to his love of power.

The unexpected opposition he met with in his enterprise against Russia, on which he had not calculated,
but which the force of circumstances opposed to his
erroneous plans, had caused an agreement among the
Powers which did not exist in the earlier wars with
the Republic and the French Empire, and which Napoleon had thought unattainable.

That the fatal result to Napoleon of the campaign
in Russia did not deceive the Emperor Francis as to
the difficulty of attaining for the Continent a secure
political peace, events have shewn. That the political
rebuilding required after Napoleon's fall would be a
most difficult task was evident to the Emperor and

myself. In our views and feelings, the rejection of all undertakings founded merely on sentiment predominated so strongly as to give to the work whose forerunners were the victories of the Alliance, and whose result was the Peace of Paris, the same impress of quiet deliberation, which had marked our course in the preliminary period.

There was no doubt that if the Congress confined itself to the limits of calm calculation, it would be exposed to great opposition. The longest time of political peace which Europe has ever enjoyed would, however, suffice to tranquillise the conscience of the great monarch and his assistant, even if the work of the Congress itself had not remained triumphantly fireproof in the years 1848 and 1849!

The history of the Hundred Days was but an episode, in illustration of which I will relate only the following incident :—

When Napoleon, after his return to Paris, restored to Fouché his former position as Minister of Police, the latter followed exactly in the footsteps of his old course of action, which was a strange mixture of abject subjection to the views of the Emperor and of rebellion against them. Fouché, who undeniably had great insight into the position of Napoleon and of France, as well as that of the great Powers, and who saw no prospect of final victory in the return of Napoleon to the French Imperial throne, sent to me at Vienna a secret agent, with a proposal, addressed to the Emperor Francis, to proclaim the King of Rome Emperor, and accompanied also with a request addressed to myself to despatch a commissioner to Basle, to come to an arrangement for the carrying out of the project. How abhorrent such a step as this would be to the Emperor

Francis, on this the French Minister of Police alone could entertain any delusion. The Emperor commanded me at once to communicate the proposal to the Emperor Alexander and King Frederick William, and to leave it to their judgment, not whether the idea should be entertained, but whether a confidential agent should be despatched to obtain information with respect to the proposal. Both monarchs advised this step. I commissioned an official of my department to undertake this business, informed him of the secret password, and bade him hear everything and say nothing. The agents met at an appointed hour, and after a short time separated because neither had anything to communicate to the other. It afterwards came out that Napoleon had been informed of the step of his Minister of Police, and instead of a representative of Fouché's, had sent to Basle an agent of his own. This history has found its way into the memoirs of the time, and originated a report of an understanding between Napoleon and the Emperor Francis. Thus is history written!

The battle of Waterloo gave the finishing stroke to the destiny of Napoleon. Even if this battle had not resulted in the success due to the iron resolution of the English General and the courageous assistance of Field-Marshal Blücher, the cause of Napoleon would nevertheless have been irretrievably lost. The Austrian and Russian armies together, with the contingent of the German Confederation, moving towards the Rhine, would have spread over France. The power which she before possessed under the Empire was completely broken in consequence of the destructive concessions which Napoleon in the course of the Hundred Days was constrained to make. Bonapartism lived only in the army and with some adherents among the civilians. The

country sighed for peace in 1815 as it had sighed for
it in preceding years. If the character of Louis XVIII.
had been different, the house of Bourbon would have
lasted longer than it did. My feeling in this respect
was not the product of a later time : I held it after the
first return of Louis XVIII. and briefly expressed it to
the King himself in these words : *Votre Majesté croit
fonder la Monarchie: Elle se trompe, c'est la Révolution
qu'Elle prend en sous-œuvre!*

I took the liberty of reminding the King of this
remark, after his second return. Louis XVIII. was
gifted with much power of mind, which, however, took
rather a theoretical than a practical direction. He
ascended the throne in 1814, still under the influence of
those views which had caused him to play the part of
president of a section of the *Assemblée des Notables*. To
these he had added some ideas, gathered, during his
emigration, from the *école anglaise*, of the same kind as
those which since Montesquieu's time had perplexed so
many minds in France.

The second Peace of Paris was the complement of
the first, and differed from it only in this, that the
Powers desired to give to the country a lesson, by taking
away some places on the frontier, by restoring to foreign countries the art-treasures seized in the wars of
the Revolution, by imposing a contribution, and by the
temporary occupation of some of the departments, in
order to secure internal peace and the safety of the
ancient throne of France.

During the negotiations of the second Peace of Paris,
the Emperor Alexander desired me to come to him, that
he might impart to me that he was occupied with a
great undertaking, about which he wished especially to
consult the Emperor Francis. 'There are things,' said

the Emperor, 'which feelings must decide, and feelings are under the influence of personal position and situation. These have a commanding influence on individuals. If it was a matter of business, I should ask you for your advice, but the present matter is of such a kind that not the ministers but only the monarchs are capable of deciding it. Tell the Emperor Francis that I wish to speak to him on a subject on which I can explain myself only to him. It will then be in his power to take counsel of you, my dear Prince.'

After a lapse of some days, I was summoned by the Emperor Francis, who told me that early on that day he had called upon the Emperor Alexander in consequence of a request from him for a personal interview on a most important subject. ' You will learn,' said his Majesty, ' what the subject is from this document, which he committed to my careful consideration. You know I do not like to express myself on a subject which I have not thoroughly examined. I have therefore taken this paper, which is written in the Emperor Alexander's own hand, and reserved to myself the power of expressing an opinion upon it. Read and examine it, and tell me your opinion of the document, which does not please me at all; it has indeed excited the most grave reflections in my mind.'

No very severe examination was required on my part to see that the paper was nothing more than a philanthropic aspiration clothed in a religious garb, which supplied no material for a treaty between the monarchs, and which contained many phrases that might even have given occasion to religious misconstructions.

On the projected treaty, therefore, my views coincided with those of the Emperor Francis; and as the Emperor Alexander had told the Emperor Francis that the document was to be shown to the King of Prussia, his Majesty ordered me to go to the King and ask his opinion of it. I found the King also agreed with the Emperor Francis, except that he hesitated to reject the views of the Russian monarch entirely. However, we came to an agreement as to the impossibility of executing the document without some absolutely necessary changes in the text. Even to this the Emperor Francis did not quite agree.

In consequence of this, I was charged by both monarchs to go to the Emperor Alexander as their common representative. In a conversation of several hours, I succeeded, not without great difficulty, in persuading the author of the necessity of changing several sentences and omitting some passages entirely.

I gave his Majesty, my Imperial master, an account of the objections which I had made without reserve about this, at any rate, useless scheme, and of my prediction of the malicious interpretation which I felt certain it would not escape.

The Emperor Francis, although he did not approve the project even when modified, agreed to sign it, for reasons which I for my part could not oppose.

This is the history of the ' Holy Alliance,' which even in the partial feeling of its originator had no other object than that of a moral demonstration, whilst in the eyes of the other persons concerned the document had no such meaning, and therefore does not deserve the interpretation which was afterwards put on it by party spirit.

The most unanswerable proof of the correctness of this statement exists in the circumstance that never afterwards did it happen that the ' Holy Alliance ' was made mention of between the cabinets, nor indeed could it have been mentioned. Only the parties hostile to the monarchs used it as a weapon for the calumniation of the purest intentions of their opponents.

The 'Holy Alliance' was not an institution to keep down the rights of the people, to promote absolutism or any other tyranny. It was only the overflow of the pietistic feeling of the Emperor Alexander, and the application of Christian principles to politics.

From a union of religious and political-liberal ideas the 'Holy Alliance' was developed under the influence of Frau von Krüdener and Monsieur Bergasse. No one is so well acquainted as I am with the circumstances of this 'loud-sounding nothing.'

In conclusion, I may be allowed to throw a passing glance over the Austrian Monarchy, and to give in a few lines the picture of a country which to foreigners has always had the character of a *terra incognita*.

The kingdom, which only since 1806 has taken the name of the Austrian Empire, is like no other either in its origin or its maturity. To the Ostmark of the Empire many other districts have been added under the House of Hapsburg, which were formerly separated from each other by history or nationality. These have brought to this dynasty in the course of generations a great possession, not, with few exceptions, by way of conquest, but by hereditary succession, contracts of marriage, and voluntary submission with reservation of individual rights. That these rights and reservations were generally maintained by the rulers, when they were not forfeited by single portions of the Empire, is a truth which the party spirit and political strife of foreigners may attack but can never destroy. If this may be maintained in general of the rulers of the House of Hapsburg, the reign of the Emperor Joseph II. is an exception in the history of Austria, the consequences of which, so far from answering the expectations of that monarch, have led the kingdom and the government into difficulties in exact opposition to his intentions.

From the singular formation of the whole kingdom, united under a succession of rulers unbroken for centuries, arose the extraordinary want of a name for this whole—a want which is shown by its appellation of the ' House of Hapsburg,' or the 'House of Austria.' This case is unique in the history of states, for in no other country has the name of the ruling family been used instead of the name of the country in ordinary, and still less in diplomatic, usage. Not until 1806, at the same time with the extinction of the German Imperial dignity, did the Emperor Francis give to his Empire the name of the ' Empire of Austria,' which appellation was not chosen arbitrarily, but was a necessity, and gave the appearance as if the parts were united to the whole and to each other only by a personal union.

The coronation of the Emperor should form the keystone of the new edifice. This design was executed in the Patent of 1806, but, from the circumstances of the times, not carried into effect. Subsequently there were two moments when this omission might have been repaired : first, the General Peace ; secondly, at the accession of the first successor to the Founder of the Austrian Empire. Both times I raised my voice in favour of the coronation. According to my views, deputations from all parts of the monarchy should assist at the coronation, thus performing an act of common homage to the common head of the State, whilst they should receive the assurance of the maintenance of the constitutional rights of each country.

The Empire of Austria, without being a federal

state, had yet the advantage and the disadvantage of a federal constitution. If the head of the house was in the modern sense of the word absolute, this notion was restricted in its sovereign power, according to the different constitutions of the several countries whose crowns he united on his own head. That this position was a most peculiar one cannot be doubted ; and it is no less certain that it would have been untenable, if it had not been founded on the most important of motives— namely, the interest of the different parts of the Empire in being united. These facts, which were clearly seen by the Emperor and myself, exercised a decided influence on the reconstruction of the Empire in the years 1813 to 1815.

The union of the former Austrian Netherlands and of the districts known under the name of the Austrian *Vorlande* with the Austrian Empire would, in the years just mentioned, not only not have been objected to, but the re-union of Belgium with the Empire was even desired by the Allied Powers on natural political grounds. We rejected it, in consequence of a consideration, not referring to our Empire alone, but to the great work of peace. We wished to remove our country from direct contact with France, and thus put an end to the wars which had been in consequence of this contact perpetually occurring between the two neighbouring empires. For France is the country where innovations of all kinds are most easily introduced, but where old accustomed impressions last the longest. From this latter reason, the altered situation of Austria and France, after the return of the old dynasty to the French throne, was not noticed either by the public or even in the cabinet, and there was in many minds the same idea of wars between France and Austria as if the geographical position of the two countries was the same as in the times of Francis I. and Louis XIV.

The Act of Congress had placed the possessions of the kingdom and the states on firm foundations. The four Powers which had so successfully driven back France into her old boundaries, admitted the French crown into their alliance replaced in its former rights. From the Quadruple Alliance, dissolved in consequence of its political end being attained, arose the moral Pentarchy, whose power was afterwards established, limited, and regulated in the Congress of Aix-la-Chapelle.

Thus the foundations of a lasting Peace were secured as far as possible.